May You be encouraged and inspired.

AN EAR TO HEAR
A GUIDE FOR THE LAITY

by
SUSTAH MAGGIE

1663 LIBERTY DRIVE, SUITE 200
BLOOMINGTON, INDIANA 47403
(800) 839-8640
WWW.AUTHORHOUSE.COM

This book is a work of non-fiction. Unless otherwise noted, the author and the publisher make no explicit guarantees as to the accuracy of the information contained in this book and in some cases, names of people and places have been altered to protect their privacy.

© 2005 SUSTAH MAGGIE. All Rights Reserved.

No part of this book may be reproduced, stored in a retrieval system, or transmitted by any means without the written permission of the author.

First published by AuthorHouse 05/26/05

ISBN: 1-4208-4916-6 (sc)

*Printed in the United States of America
Bloomington, Indiana*

This book is printed on acid-free paper.

ACKNOWLEDGMENTS

All thanks to our Father-God for His love and saving grace that lead me into serving His people of Kenya. Then I want to thank my precious sister/friend Jean and my children who embraced this assignment as a family mission.

I am grateful for my spiritual daughter Grace, and fellow-servant, Rosemary Gathaiya (my angel); many thanks to the Illinois Mount Joy M.B. Church choir; thanks to my niece Minister Colbert, Bishop T. Benjamin and LWCC for their enormous help to move the work forward in Kibera.

Special gratitude and thanks to Sister Denise and Mrs. Hilda Nolte, and to Bishop J. B. Ransom of Dallas. Words can not fully express how much I appreciate the many known and anonymous education sponsors that made the success of the Sponsorship Program possible.

I am deeply grateful for Chris and Violet who opened their hearts to share their vision, and allowed me to have a role in it.

Foremost, I thank God for Mr. Murage and his editor for their willingness to assist me, and literally gave my efforts a jumpstart in Kenya.

God will let the record show how each one of you carried the cross of the Kibera Mission to victory, and whatsoever is right, He will reward you.

Contents

ACKNOWLEDGMENTS v
INTRODUCTION ix
1. CONFLICTS WITH COMMON SENSE..............................1
2. A DEFINED MISSION 19
3. AS I SAT WHERE THEY SAT..29
4. MAKING HISTORY 37
5. TRANSFORMING LIVES..57
6. WHILE DESTINY PREVAILED 69
7. WHEN IT MIRRORS UGLINESS...85
8. ANGELS ACCOMPLISHED THEIR PURPOSE 89
9. CONCLUSION GREAT NEWS FOR THE UNNOTICED ...99
APPENDIX...103

INTRODUCTION

This is a story about love, communication and purpose given by the Father-God, without partiality. This unconditional love provides equal opportunity for all His sons and daughters to talk to Him and to hear from Him, collectively and individually.

<u>An Ear to Hear</u> emphasizes that in God's hands, little is much; our weakness brings forth His supernatural strength. This story tells how God used a single word to create a taskforce made up of strangers on four continents, through which He moved mightily in behalf of indigent families and destitute children. This hand-picked team was to serve those, apparently, forgotten by their government and forsaken by the church; their mission was spoken into existence with one word: ***NAIROBI***

In and outside of the United States, I have met those who believe a revelation from God should be either preceded or accompanied by a grandiose display of lightning, being slain in the spirit or periods of speaking in unknown tongues. With the single word "NAIROBI" God carved out nearly six years of my life, and sent me to tend to His lambs of another fold.

A young Kenyan journalist once asked me, "Just how does God's voice sound?" Among the laity where I have traveled, men, women, seniors and the young, have expressed the resounding concern: "I want to fulfill my purpose in God, but how can I know when it is really God speaking?"

For this reason, I felt that the time had come to share my story with those already knowledgeable about the many ways God communicates with His people, but particularly, I hope to offer a guide and reassurance to the laity who desires an enriched relationship with the Lord.

An Ear to Hear testifies to how God is not restricted to a set pattern or method; God knows best how to speak to the heart, and to cause us to know His will. Through my assignment to Kenya, I found that being given 'an ear to hear' came with an awesome responsibility to God, my neighbor and myself.

Let me make it clear, I was not born a gifted, better than the average or halo-crowned child. However, the earliest message from God to me came in Matthews 19:14, when I was six-years-old, just learning how to read, and did not know that God Almighty talks to little kids. It took 40 years for that scripture to unfold into a bigger picture—a greater move—far-reaching into the Kenya slums of the Kibera Village.

Across my adult life, the various communications that I had with the Lord was indicative to being given a gift–the gift of an ear to hear. In this story, it is evident that to hear from our Father is not a mammoth task, if we continue in the way that He leads.

1. CONFLICTS WITH COMMON SENSE

"For my thoughts are not your thoughts..."
Isaiah 55:8 (AKJV)

Despite their pot-bellies, unwashed scantily dressed bodies and running noses, children of Kibera still had dreams for a brighter future. Each day, this served as the only motivation I had to cross the railroad tracks, walk down the slippery slope to the school and to endure the stench.

As one used to city life, it took much skill to maneuver my way around the goats and chickens then avoid human and animal excrement, sewage-filled slush in stomach-churning squalor. While it happened, I knew the children of the village waited to get a glimpse of me slosh my way on the murky trail, alongside the Kibera River.

A few yards from the school, the alleged 'dumping ground' for amputated limbs from the Kenyatta National Hospital, heightened the pollution. Nevertheless, since I had become headmistress in 1989, the Kibera Soweto School enrollment had swollen and the waiting list had grown.

More fortunate Kenyans (up to fifty-years-old), even the most devout Christians, would not have dared to set foot in what appeared to be a God-forsaken area and they had never seen the place. This was precisely where God had work to be done; He assigned my hands to help do the job.

As I walked to the school, my thoughts converged on events that led me to the Kenya village and the fledgling elementary school. It all started in March 1986.

I received this commission to Kibera through a *veiled* message of just one word: **NAIROBI.** Twenty-years of single parenting had trained me; prepared my heart to look beyond what the naked eye can see and my ears to hear what was not audible to others.

On that Saturday morning when it happened, the word **'NAIROBI'** stood blocking my efforts to pray and it did not go away, until I asked a crucial question: "Lord, are you telling me to go there?"

Immediately, these instructions were given: **PAY OFF ALL DEBTS, LEAVE NOTHING OWING; STUDY TO LEARN ALL YOU CAN; ARRANGE TO BE THERE FROM FIVE TO SEVEN YEARS; PREPARE YOUR HEARTS**

FOR SEPARATION; YOU HAVE NOTHING TO LOSE, EVERYTHING TO GAIN.

At the end of our prayer, my armpits were moist; questions danced in my mind; exhaustion made it difficult to rise from my knees and sit on the bedside. The mental and physical fatigue was much like the result of a championship wrestlers' match.

My middle daughter Yvonne was the only one present with me, after the prayer, she listened to me in astonishment. I tried to explain to her the one thing of which there were no doubts–God had spoken.

"I believe that God is sending me to Nairobi Kenya," I said with bated breath.

At that point, no clue was revealed as to *why* I had to go, but I told her what had occurred while we were on our knees. As the 24-year-old looked at me in amazement but not in disbelief; she, too, explained a realization she had felt within her heart, while we were in prayer.

"I sensed that you were no longer in this room, Mom, although I don't know where you were in spirit." She asserted, "You left me alone in this room for awhile."

How many times through the media have we heard someone say '**God told me**,' whether in the church or outside the spiritual realm? In a broad scope, wars are fought sometimes because one of the opponents, or both, claim that they are following God's orders. Sadly, some in our society who are deranged have even murdered; allegedly, they have claimed that 'God told them to do it.'

Could it be that such claims are often indiscriminately prefaced with '**God told me...**' because it can be said without proof or subsequent evidence? Without benefit of a trained *listening ear* of the clergy, could an ordinary lay person have an "ear to hear" God's voice? Like others, I believed that to converse with God is for a privileged few.

For the above reasons, skepticism that I faced could be easily understood when I first said that God told me to go to Africa. Despite my having no background in seminary studies or benefit to work alongside a notable church leader, what was GOD thinking?

Relatives and friends had legitimate concerns, for which I had no *logical* replies. "Is your job with the governor's office sending you?" *No.* "Do you have a job there already?" *No.* "So you're quitting your good job to go where you'll have no visible support, and you expect us to believe that **God toldya todoit**?"

When that assignment to East Africa was initially given, I readily recall that common sense pointed me in other directions. My only certainty was that the *Lord* had spoken, because long before this occurred I had received the gift of **an ear to hear.**

At first, family members treated it as a joke, basically, they dismissed the issue; friends showed grave concern for my mental stability. To them, vague responses to their questions gave credence to 'something' being wrong with my ability to reason. Through worldly wisdom some said, 'lots of women go through mid-life crises, after their children are grown—and gone.'

Janet, my dearest friend/oldest sister and sister in Christ felt perplexed about the whole thing; we both dreaded our pending separation. She, too, expressed her concern.

"Why is God sending you so far away from your family, and for so long?"

I replied, "Maybe because I owe so much." At the same time, I wondered if this had been planned for my life, before I begin to realize it.

I asked the Lord, "What should I tell my children?" Only one explanation was given me to offer them: *'I must work the work of Him that sent me.'*

Support for my personal necessities was to come from my two sons and three daughters. God said, **"As you give up here, I will provide for you there, and will especially bless those who are allowed to get involved in the work assigned to you."**

However, in a few weeks, I felt harried by inward doubts. I wondered why God had given me a foreign mission when several people, I knew, were much more qualified for the job. Other times, I thought there was nothing useful that I had to offer. Long hours spent in the library provided information about the country, and I bought books on Kenya and the national language Kiswahili.

In addition, unknown to me, resentment had ignited within my home church. Among themselves, officials questioned *just who does she think she is?* If I was to go on a mission without being assigned or approved by the religious chain-of-command, this would amount to blatant disrespect in not being subject to the authority of the church.

One leader said, "The Bible teaches that Jesus sent disciples out two-by-two, not one running off alone on an individual quest." Such action was practically unforgivable.

"In that case," I asked, "does it still require 120 people to be in an upper room, praying at the same time, in order for one person to receive the Holy Spirit?"

Thereafter, church leaders distanced themselves from the matter, and considered that this move was '*not of the Lord.*' The criteria those elders and officials used to determine that God had not spoken to me, I do not know. Conceivably, they saw me as too 'ordinary,' with no recognizable talent to bring credit to the church.

"There is a way which seemeth right unto a man..."
Prov. 14:12 (AKJV)

It was now clearer to me why God did not instruct me to seek sponsorship from organizations or churches. Before long, I soon learned that my religious affiliation was not even registered in Kenya, but our Foreign Mission leader gave me addresses for two Americans who were married to Kenyan men. In order to move forward, I wrote to the woman in Kisumu and the other that lived in Nairobi.

In the weeks ahead, something strange began to happen; my prayer life seemed to change. Deep within, it felt like I was in the presence of villagers who prayed in a language unknown to me. I felt a belonging or kinship with them. Inside, it seemed like my spirit had gone ahead and left my body behind to *mechanically* finish up the final relocation tasks.

For the past four years, I had enjoyed a coveted job, participated in civic events and unofficially represented my boss at community functions. My youngest daughter would soon be a university graduate, and I had waited long to see no more baby bottles, baby-sitters, PTA's, and due bills for school tuition.

I thought *it's my time now,* not realizing that my future faced reconstructive surgery, as priorities for my family became painstakingly rearranged. The more I prepared to depart, the stronger enticements lured me in other directions.

My niece felt that if I wanted to work out of the country, at least, I should look for a job that offered a salary. A husband and wife team at her church put a request in their Sunday Bulletin for a secretary to work with them in the Philippines; the job offered a salary and free lodging. My niece sent details and urged me to accept, if offered the job.

It made 'good sense' and it was a rational thing to do. I sent them my application, although I had mixed feelings about it. Since I was not a member of their church, I felt they might not select me and it eased my conscience, for the moment. However, within a week, I received a call in my office from the husband and we arranged to meet for lunch and do the interview then.

On the day we met, it was a pleasure to meet Mr. and Mrs. Gutenberg. She, a white American, and he a German took turns to explain their work to me. When it was time for me to tell about myself, I made no mention of Kenya.

Afterwards, I gave little thought to it but in just three days, Mr. Gutenberg telephoned to offer me the job. Instead of being delighted that they had chosen me, it left me saddened. The fact that the salary had not been discussed at the interview provided me with a good excuse to decline.

Mr. Gutenberg asked me to give him time to discuss it with his wife, and he would soon call me back. I *knew* that Nairobi was where I belonged; an avalanche of shame and guilt appeared to smother me. The Gutenberg's ministry should not have me on board as a 'prodigal Jonah' and I felt compelled to tell them about my call to Kenya. Both of them graciously wished me well, and asked that I would keep in touch.

Thank God! We're not our own. I shutter to think how, if left on my own, I would ignorantly plunge into *busyness,* thinking it's **for**

the Lord. All the time, God wants vessels **through which He may work** to accomplish His purpose.

† † † † †

Have there been times when your spirit was willing, but human intellect kept you from fully complying with God's plan? Periodically, I would look forward to a mission in Kenya in *a 30-day crusade*; a five- to seven-year stay was hard for me to imagine.

The letters sent to Kenya brought me a glimmer of hope. One woman had said in her letter, *'I urge you to make sure of your calling to Kenya because it is neither an easy life, nor a place worthy of leaving amenities in the United States to come there.'* I so appreciated her sound advice.

A breakthrough came from the lady in Nairobi. Her letter told about Barbara Jones, an American missionary who lived alone in a big house in Nairobi but needed someone to help with expenses. Like pieces to a large puzzle, every effort brought me closer to the bigger picture.

That same day, I sent a letter to Ms. Jones to explain my situation, and to ask about living arrangements. Simply put, however, I explained that my purpose for coming had not, as yet, been made clear to me, but suggested that she call me for a more personal discussion. This way, the realities of our sharing close living quarters were examined.

Months later, indecisiveness still haunted me. I made a feeble effort at becoming debt free; $200 was paid on one bill, but I charged $80-$90 on another. Something that happened made it quite clear to me that NAIROBI was a **mission without an option.**

As summer of '87 ended, a health problem grew progressively worse and sent me rushing to my gynecologist. Several tests and a second opinion revealed that I had cancer; immediate surgery was required.

On the day of the post-operative checkup, I left the office with the doctor's words echoing in my mind.

"We caught it in time. Had we waited any longer," the doctor said, "the outcome would have been critical; maybe too late."

Then I distinctly heard these sobering words from the Lord, "**If there was not a mission for you in Kenya, your encounter with cancer would have been fatal.**"

Yes, time had been allowed to rear my children; time permitted for sufficient preparation; time to make certain my calling; time for the Holy Spirit to pull down strong holds on *imagined rights* and *presumed privileges.* Time for me to decide what I would or would **not do** had expired. The remaining time now, indeed, belonged to the Lord.

Early in my Christian life, I had a favorite scripture:

> **"... Whom shall I send, and who will go for us?..."**
> **Isaiah 6:8 (KJV).**

As often as it was read, I had mouthed the same response, (basically figurative), *Lord, I'll go; You can use me anytime, any where.* Now it appeared that God's reply was, 'Let's see.'

Quite often, as Christians, we make promises to the Lord. As time slips pass us and we might not remember it, He calls on us to keep a promise. At a time least expected, I had to let go of most material gains and relationships had to be severed.

During my convalescence, Barbara Jones answered my letter to say that she needed help not only with expenses, but with her spiritual work as well. Also, she promised to have a pastor in Kenya, with whom she worked, to contact me and to assist in any way possible.

As living in Kenya gradually became realizable, glimpses of our past struggles—in short flashes—went back to when I was a young divorcee. Since half of the sixties and across the seventies decades, our struggle to maintain harmony and togetherness among the six of us had salvaged our lives. A nine-year turbulent marriage ended in 1964, and this sent the perils of single parenting to greet me at every turn.

With four children and pregnant with the fifth, I was inexperienced in managing outside the home. In that era, if statistics held true regarding broken homes, then society had a disintegrating future waiting for us, but as it happened, I felt driven to knit my family closer together. I longed to find a way to help my children to keep **out of jail and off drugs, and avoid unwed pregnancies, especially while in their teen years.**

Calm and quiet appearances gave little warning that seething upheaval would soon slither underneath our front door. It was unusual to see a family headed by a man, and living in a predominately female environment offered my sons little persuasion to confidently function as men.

An application to the Big Brothers Organization in behalf of my sons proved to be unsuccessful. Few African American men registered with them, because all effort and time had to be given for survival of their own family.

The high hopes I held for the success of my family began to dwindle, but if we succumbed to the pressures, I knew the 'streets' waited with open arms to engulf my children. I felt haunted by that fear day and night; I could not imagine life without them.

Caught in the undercurrent, my family began to lose something valuable that money could not buy. The harder I worked and the more I purchased, the more we seemed to lose; our home life plummeted. Although we were active in church programs, none directly addressed the critical crises that single parents faced.

Not so apparent was that my own behavior began to change; hate for our environment and bitterness welled up inside me. We were economically deprived on the outside, threatened by family turbulence within, and at times, I reeked with self-pity.

Tormented by the possibility that my kids might run away, as thousands of American youth did in that era, I believed that, inevitably, we would lose one another.

Still, I found myself shouting at the children, and would also beat them out frustration. Despair, guilt and fear held me in a paralytic grip.

Soaked in depression, I contemplated suicide and started to think that my kids may be better off without me. In my belief that this deterioration was against God's design for families then He, alone, could give a solution, I prayed and asked for a cohesive family-plan. Before a week passed, it appeared that our plan began with a simple act; in a business style, I mailed postcards addressed to each child in his or her own name.

You have an appointment with Ms. Cason
Time: 3:30 – 4:30 P.M.
Date: March 05, 1969
Where: Her Room-upstairs
Please bring any complaints or suggestions you may have.

Notices were mailed at the first of the month; no more than two children were scheduled a day, at different times. The eleven-year old had one hour; nine-year olds, forty-five minutes each; the seven-year old, half an hour and the three-year old was given fifteen minutes. I was not sure how they would react as the cards first arrived in the mail, and the reaction caught me off guard. The oldest boy gleefully read his card aloud.

"Oh! Mama, I got mail in my very own name—jest like grown people git."

He helped the others to read their cards; it captured all their attention. Reactions exceeded my expectations. We met at their given times, respectively; growing interest exuded through their conversations and a sense of expectancy began to flow.

As time went by, one would say, "I have a good suggestion to make in my conference with Mama," or "I got ideas ready for my next meeting."

When the first month of talks ended, any skepticism they had had was over-shadowed by their anticipation. Without my prodding or questioning, freedom of expression was established and confidentiality was maintained, much like that of priest and parishioner in Confession. Understanding and trust was our goal; it would set the precedence for how we should deal with more crucial issues later.

Even the middle children received undivided attention; without embarrassment, each youngster began to ask questions on subjects usually avoided with parents. It did not take long before they would continue a discussion 10-15 minutes beyond their time.

The lesson I learned was that no role is greater than that of the parent to influence a child's future. At the onset, our family had

stood on the edge of a teetering future, wi[...]
therapy or other costly methods. After b[...]
many social pitfalls, we won.

More often than not, with no second c[...]
destroys the root.

After high school, my oldest son declin[...]
and was recruited into the U.S. Air For[...]
rending to let go of him, but there were fo[...]
twin son decided he was ready for his independence.

At three different occasions, the youngest son earnestly tried to make it on his own. Each time, however, the 21-year-old returned home, sometimes, for reasons beyond his control. This chain of events caused a complete turnabout in our family because up to then, all efforts had been focused on cohesion.

Realities of life made us look deeper into some of the problems that confronted young adults caught in the move-out process. We discovered that it could be a most discouraging feat for the young trying to face life on their own.

First, without former landlords' reference, apartment managers seldom risked renting to young people. Second, the furniture and utility companies had the same requirements; namely, large deposits and down payments, established credit accounts and three to five years of stable employment.

Instead of their leaving home, I decided to move because my manageability could better balance the odds. Three oldest that yet lived at home had full time employment; up to that time, they never knew how much utilities cost a month, or when bills were due.

My leaving would provide them a furnished place with utilities on, and an opportunity for responsible budgeting. They arranged a three-way split of house and food expense—all of which had been previously paid out of my salary alone. Also, it presented them with the chance to start a Personal Savings Account, and small items could be purchased to establish a line of credit.

At this point in our lives, my role was needed just to gauge how well my sons and daughters made the transition into self-governed independence. Therefore, in 1981 I moved away from my home to apartment, leased for one year. I took my Bible, clothes ...g machine, along with best wishes from my children.

...e Saturday out of every month, we held a lunch meeting in my ...tment, at which time they gave me payment receipts, because ...ccounts were still in my name. I found that they were handling their responsibility in a conscientious manner.

Four of them acquired a minimal of 13 years of schooling. We had no smokers, drugs or alcohol users; no parents or abortions; no arrests, especially in their teen years.

As we entered our third year of living apart, the Saturday family prayer started; in the next two years, the East Africa assignment was given. Time had come for our hands to reach out to people of another culture, and God had not given us a list of choices.

† † † † †

While in preparation to leave family and country, a surge of encouragement came when a letter arrived from Pastor Paul of Nairobi. He assured me that he would make my coming to Kenya "less complicated" and he would help me to get settled, once I arrived.

January 1988, things began to happen fast. I had returned to work in a different frame of mind, and soon confirmed my flight to Africa via London. As bills were paid, I cut up credit cards. The dreaded, but necessary immunizations began, and I packed only bare necessities; mostly, loose fitting cotton clothing and eliminated the suits and furs.

September '88 marked my last day at work and the end of a regular salary. A letter with all my travel details and arrival time was mailed to Pastor Paul. It would take about ten days for him to get the information, and time enough to arrange to meet me at the airport. If he could foresee any problems then he could inform me, before I left.

On the eve of my departure, I spent the night with Yvonne. However, mental entanglement of conflicting loyalties and desires kept me awake through the night. The next morning, as I prepared to leave, I put the left arm in my jacket sleeve but pulled the other side over my shoulder leaving the right sleeve empty.

In her mothering manner, Yvonne asked, "Can you please tell me why you're wearing your jacket like that?" She tried to make sure that nothing went wrong.

I said, "Because I'm leaving you—my right arm—behind in the States." As I fought back tears I added, "I'll put it on at the airport."

I had sternly refused anyone to come to see me off at the airport; nagging doubts were already hard to contend with about going into unfamiliar territory. As I reached for the door knob, I heard the quivering voice of Yvonne singing the Lionel Richie's song: "You're Once, Twice, Three Times a Lady, and I lov . . ."

No further words came, as both of us wept and embraced, not knowing just when we would meet again, or if the five to seven years meant no visit home in between.

Once aboard the plane, I realized that Pastor Paul had sent no reply to my latest letter, but I forced away all thoughts and slept.

October 30, 1988, my TWA Flight arrived 5:55 A.M. at Heathrow and I found my son and his wife waiting to greet me. It was my first visit to London, but very little stuck in my mind about that visit. During the five-day stay on the Air Force Base, one of my son's buddies questioned him about me.

He said, "Just how do you feel about your mom going to a place where she hasn't been before, and has no family there—to Africa, of all places?"

My son replied, "When we were growing up and Mom said that God told her to do something, we saw results. So if she says that God told her to go to Kenya, I have no problem with that, but I don't understand why it has to be so long."

It was a cold dismal day as we started our drive to Gatwick Airport to catch the 10:30 A.M. flight on British Airlines. Once aboard the aircraft, I first sat on the edge with seatbelts in both hands. Vacillation burst forth with fears and doubts.

The enemy made this case: 'What will you do when you arrive and nobody is at the airport to meet you? You don't know their language and they don't know yours. How will you manage without someone to help you? There is yet time to deplane and catch your son before he leaves the airport.'

While attendants secured overhead compartments, I sat frozen with seatbelt unfastened, until I heard a voice that soothed my nerves.

"Is Your God One that will send you somewhere and leave you stranded?" The Holy Spirit asked then answered, **"He has never been known to turn His back."**

It was settled. I slid back, fastened the belt and made myself content for the nine-hour flight, scheduled to arrive about six o'clock a.m., Kenya time. I tried to imagine what the family was thinking, but another question dominated my wake hours:

What was so urgent in Kenya that required my whole life to be altered?

November 6, the flight landed at Jomo Kenyatta Airport at 6:30 A.M., and when I finally cleared customs, it felt good to have my feet on Nairobi soil. My apprehension increasingly grew as to what might happen.

With a deep-breath sigh, I walked out to greet a stormy Sunday morning laced with swift warm winds. Some people held up placards with English names, others had African names, but none had mine. I pushed the cart heavily loaded with luggage and slowly strolled, as the crowd of 187 passengers began to thin.

Suddenly, I heard this question: "Are you Sustah Maggie?" A man said in a low and timid voice then added, "I'm Pastor Paul Juma."

Whew! Never before had I been so glad to hear my own name. I whirled around and flashed a broad smile to the thin, medium height man standing near me.

As we stood face to face, I said in relief, "Y-yes, I am. You came! Thank God, You're here!"

"Amen! Yes, my Sustah, we are six who have come here to greet you—WELCOME to Kenya," he warmly expressed in recognizable English.

The Pastor looked to be in his forties and brought five brothers from his church; four of which spoke English very well. After introductions, we headed to the car and they loaded the luggage. To my surprise, all seven of us would travel in one vehicle.

Wipers and lights on the old derelict Toyota did not function, but one brother attempted to keep the windscreen cleared by hand. Smoke from the car motor indicated that a miracle was needed to get us out of airport parking.

Any uncertainty I felt was due to the condition of the car and weather, rather than my aloneness with six male strangers in a country unknown to me. Lack of familiarity was more like moving into a new neighborhood, and not at all like an alien.

Through God's mercy, by ten o'clock, we drove into the city area where someone suggested that we stop for hamburgers at a Burger King. Another brother said that it would be his treat to all of us.

Pastor Paul mentioned that Sister Barbara had traveled to the States, but he felt that she had already returned, anticipating my coming. Soon after the food was put on the table, four of the brothers decided to go to check things out, and find out if Sister Barbara had come back to Nairobi.

The Fanta soda, at room temperature, was the way most Kenyans preferred it, regardless to the 20c temperature. I tried to tactfully express concern that the guys had driven off with every piece of clothing I had, but was assured that all was "very safe."

Nearly two hours later, we were still sitting in the restaurant and Pastor Paul tried to keep me busy in answering trivial things they asked about the United States. Instead, my concentration remained on the four who left with the luggage, and I had no clue where they were, or if they would return. I inquired again for the fourth time.

"Where are those guys with my bags?" I said, but this time, the answer given would become a hard lesson for me to learn, for my entire stay in Kenya.

"My Sustah," the young pastor said with a wide grin, "we say here that *there are no clocks in Kenya*, please don't worry because I expect they'll be back in an hour or so."

Another hour! I thought, but tried not to become alarmed. At 1:30 p.m., two of the men returned to the restaurant, wearing broad smiles. The men that remained with me appeared calm, and took

SUSTAH MAGGIE

no notice of the ones coming back to our tables. Brother Waihenya spoke first.

"Well-ll, we have come. In fact, we found that our Sustah Barbara returned to Nairobi just two days ago."

"But where is my luggage?" I could wait no longer, "is it still in the car?"

"Nooo!" Brother Okumu said, "All your things were left at the house in your room, as Sustah Barbara insisted. In fact, she is waiting for us to bring you there straightaway—even as we speak," he said.

I managed to strain out a nervous grin, as a tinge of excitement came over me. We left for the Buru Buru Estates, in which I hoped to call home, for the next five to seven years. We arrived at house #45Z, with a brown Toyota parked in the front yard. The front of the house had an iron, grill type door on the outside; a thick wooden door inside that stood ajar.

As the five of us got out of the car, a 5'5" brown-skinned, middle-aged woman opened up the iron-grill door. She had a pleasant face, partially covered on the sides by a curly wig. The plump woman was neatly dressed in a print skirt and white blouse, and on her feet were blue cloth house slippers.

"Karibuni!" Barbara Jones welcomed us in Kiswahili and in English, "Welcome to Kenya and the work of the Lord," she said.

After she introduced herself to me, Barbara explained that she had had to make a trip home to the States and to hurry back before I arrived. She asked which one of us wanted juice to drink, or tea, then instructed us to make ourselves comfortable, as she went into the kitchen.

The two-bedroom house had a shower room with a cement floor, and an inside toilet; in the 15' x 20' sitting room was a sofa made up of three foam cushions on top of two large clothes trunks, with a clean flower print cover. The walls were painted white.

A goatskin drum, 35-inches in diameter, served as a tea table in the sitting room. Across the linoleum covered floor, in the corner near the front window, was an armed chair with a loose fitted vinyl pillow for the seat, and several folding chairs.

Barbara had tried to think of all I might need to be comfortable in the bedroom assigned to me. Clean white curtains waved in the breeze from a window on the backside of the room; about a dozen wire hangers were on the twin-sized bed, along with a light blanket. Neatly arranged was a three-legged, three feet high stool at a wooden desk, with a small table lamp made from a bottle and an electric cord extended through it.

When our snack was finished, I excused myself to go into my bedroom about 7:00 p.m., and left Paul and Barbara engaged in a discussion. After I had hung a few pieces in a built-in wall closet, fatigue completely bridled me. So I showered and went to bed. For a few hours, I slept soundly and never knew when Barbara had gone to her room.

2. A DEFINED MISSION

Approximately, 3:00 a.m. I awakened and prayed with one prevalent question on my mind: *Why was it necessary for me to come to this country?* By dawn, I sat at the desk and wrote letters to let my family know that I was safe and settled in at the house of Barbara Jones.

Although they would see some humor in it, I knew that Americans might find it hard to imagine how we managed in a storm with inoperable wipers, or how nothing was taken from my luggage in the hands of four strangers.

About nine o'clock, I could hear Barbara in the kitchen singing songs in English and some in Swahili, as she prepared breakfast. Later, she also mentioned that a friend who lived nearby would come to join us for breakfast and to meet me.

In a few minutes, a medium height, very dark skinned man came up to the door. He called out Barbara's name, opened the door for himself, and stepped into the house.

"Oh, Charles," Barbara said, "comon in here and meet Missionary Maggie; God has sent me some help." Her face beamed as she said to me, "He's like my son."

"Praise the Lawd, Sustah," he said and gave me a firm handshake.

The 33-year-old Charles began to give me his three-minute testimony, and then added that he was married. He and his wife Valerie lived a block from Barbara, around the corner. When he stopped to catch his breath and sat down to eat, I told my testimony.

"I'm also happy to say that I've been redeemed."

At first, the young man looked disappointed. I would learn later that in Kenya, a long testimony was more **believable**. Barbara had many stories of her work across the 12 years she had, intermittently, served in Kenya. I felt honored that God had given me Barbara (like an Apostle Paul with my role as Timothy) to learn from her.

Charles Otieno agreed to take Barbara to get her telephone turned back on, and he suggested it would be a good time for him to show me around the City Centre. Because it would take Barbara most of the day to take care of her business, Charles escorted me around town, showed where to get postage for foreign mail then took me to Barclay's Bank to open an account. Currency exchange was 18 shillings to U.S. dollar.

After I saw the International Conference Center, Parliament Buildings and other landmarks in Nairobi, Charles invited me to go to *Kibera* to see work God had given him.

Approximately, 10-12 miles outside the Nairobi business district, I noticed that conditions of the communities grew progressively worse, like we had entered another world. Every two minutes, Charles turned to the right or left, in order to avoid large potholes and difficult stony road passages.

"See these women sitting alongside the road," Charles explained, "they're out here early, maybe 5:00 in the morning, until its gets dark again. They get just enough money for food today; tomorrow, they have to the same thing again."

Dozens of women, of all ages, had pyramid-stacked fruits and vegetables to sell. In Kiswahili, each one boasted to have the best bargain; they sold and customers bartered.

Teenage boys had makeshift charcoal grills on which to roast maize in 1 ½ inch pieces to sell. Although the kiosks would sell one egg, half a loaf of bread, or four ounces of tealeaves, very few families could afford to buy either, in a community where charges for use of a latrine were beyond their reach.

The squalor and stench attacked my senses. Although in shock, my eyes became fixed on gross deprivations, my heart perceived far more; even then, I somehow knew that I would never be the same.

It appeared that conditions could not get worse; until we entered the Kibera Village. It was then that my eyes fastened on unimaginable poverty, and faces with hollow eyes reflecting starvation and dying hope. Undernourished adults, and hungry naked toddlers cried on the wayside, with their comfort, nutrition and smiles held hostage by failed government policies and the hard life of Africa; robbed of human dignities.

Charles stopped and parked his car upon the main road and said, "The path to the depths of the valley is impassable with a vehicle. We have to hop over muddy puddles, climb hills and duck away from running goats; I don't think you're used to such places in the U.S.—everything there looks so clean."

Shortly, we entered a dense area of one-room huts made of mud, sticks and sand, no grass was seen and the bare yards would become muddy during the rains. Soon, Charles pointed out a larger building.

"Sustah Maggie, that's my place," he said, "but as you can see, these temporary buildings made of mud deteriorate fast when long rains come. In Kibera, nobody use window glass, it costs too much and thieves would not allow it to last overnight, but shutters work fine to close up buildings. It works better to keep out thieves."

Inside the school-cum-church, twenty backless benches rowed by tens served as seats and desks for the 12 small children I saw seated in class. As we walked toward them, two young women stood up where they were sitting in wooden straight-backed chairs at a table.

Charles motioned to a podium leaned against the wall and he said that it was used for church on Sundays. He introduced me to the two teachers, and both of them spoke English well. The youngest, about 19, was first to shake my hand.

"Sustah Maggie, I'm Ruth, and I live with Pastor Charles and his wife. When I came up-country to get a job, Pastor gave me this job and a place to stay."

"Madame, you're welcome." The other lady shook my hand and said, "I'm Mrs. Achinyi and I have three children of my own. I've been with Pastor from the beginning, when he started two years ago, except for three months that Pastor did not pay any salary, so my husband made me stay home. I enjoy teaching and have a Teaching Certificate, but it is more children that need to come; parents can't afford school fees."

Later, Charles said, "Only three or four of the parents paid school fees, so the small offerings from an 18-member church–four from my house–has to supplement the school for the teachers' salaries. One day, I stood out here and I believe God was telling me that these little kids need to get an education. My wife, Valerie, and I put up something temporary to get the children started in school."

I listened intently as the young pastor told of his plans to expand the school, and the struggle it was for him to get enough money to fix a smaller back room for another class. As he talked, the Lord was also speaking to me.

"While you were talking, Pastor Charles," I said, "the Holy Spirit put it into my heart that God brought me here to help you with these children. The money you need is in the U.S., and He wants me to help you to get it."

Charles wore a look of shock, like he could not believe his ears, as I began to express what God had revealed to me. I was confident that I had to help Kibera children and suggested how it could be worked out.

"I'll reside in Nairobi, but my work is in Kibera—I know that's why God told me to come. If I could be a volunteer headmistress and manage daily activities of the school, you can take care of supplies and make sure we comply with government regulations."

Whether or not God had assigned me to be His ambassador to the Kibera children, I did not know, but the urgent need dictated where to start and left no time for hesitation.

"Praise the Laaawd! The pastor soon cut short his grin and said, "Wel-ll, what about Barbara? What I-I m-mean is… before you came, she said that you were coming to assist in her work."

"Before and after my arrival, Barbara was told that I didn't know why God wanted me in Kenya; now I do, at least, this is the main reason."

The pioneering pastor scratched his head and added, "The Assemblies of Christ (AC) can arrange for your Work Permit; you may have to pay for it, but AC will provide your coverage to work in Kenya. Barbara works with another organization of preachers."

† † † † †

After I obtained the permit, my weekdays were spent at the school from 8:30 a.m. to 2:30 p.m., but evenings and sometimes through the nights I planned, wrote letters and created necessary forms needed at the school. When I had to communicate with the parents, the teachers would interpret for me in Swahili.

One common practice in Kenya, regardless of the religious belief, children were given an African name and an English name that was called their *'Christian name.'* This custom helped me because once I learned the child's name it became easier for me to remember how to address their parents. If a girl was named Mary and her brother was named Edward, their parents could be called by either: 'Mama Mary or Mama Edward.' Likewise, the husband: Baba (father) Mary or Baba Edward.

I observed that 90% of the women wore headscarves, sandals or bare feet and no matter if the clothing was modern, old or a kanga, it was usually clean.

To move forward, I implemented a sponsorship program to get school fees for the students then mailed the announcement to family and friends in the United States. Fees would buy complete uniforms, shoes and books, and pay the teachers a regular salary.

As musician and choir director at a church in Illinois, my sister Janet quickly passed on information about the sponsorship. Between her and Yvonne, several people heard about the Kibera sponsorship initiative and, subsequently, volunteered to support it.

My arrangement with parents whose children were sponsored was that receipts for all fees should be given to me; except for sickness, the child must not be kept home to care for siblings; uniforms would be kept clean and worn only to school.

To sponsors, I promised that the child's Report Form would be mailed to them regularly to show class progress. A picture of the child dressed in full uniform would be sent, along with family profile and an annual letter from the parents.

One of our parents, Mama Monica, took education seriously for her two sons and her oldest, Monica. The teachers often remarked that Monica's hair was nicely combed.

One day Mama Monica came to talk about sponsorship, but her dilemma was difficult to explain in her little knowledge of English.

"Headmistress," she stuttered, "edkasion...impor-tont...but my job is to do foist theng foist...with no bread for my children, how can my heart separate from that? She pulled the tail of her kanga and added, "Like me, what you see on my bod-dy is all there is...maybe a person so far down as I am is not worthy for a US sponsor, I have nothing—not even the fifty cent (only pennies in US currency) for my children to use the latrine."

I said, "Mama Monica, you're not so lost in Kibera that God can't find you. Families like yours are the reason we're offering sponsorship; your kind of need is why I am here. The Lord sees all your needs. He will help in other areas—not just school."

February '89—about 90 days after my arrival, the Lord told me: **"Give a graduation for all children that finish nursery school under your leadership; give it in grand style because it would be the only graduation some of them will ever have."**

With an old manual typewriter, on loan from the Bishop of AC, I typed forms for Enrollment Applications, along with Attendance, Achievement and Hygiene Certificates.

As the teachers began to send children home with Certificates for Good Grooming, appearances of the students improved. When the parents were shown how many absent days were marked on their child's record, class attendance went up 60%.

My sister Janet and I felt that we were conjoined at the heart; through her, I learned to show love. Although she is a little older, God taught us to cultivate a friendship much like that of David and Jonathan. With her help, more sponsors became involved.

Not sixty days would pass, without my receiving a letter that began, 'Dear Sister, you don't know me, but I've heard about your work—here's a check for $20.' Another letter may have enclosed $25, or $100. The chairman of a Missionary Society at the Illinois fellowship (where Janet worked), sent $150 and wrote: 'We've decided to assist in the work you do because it's what many of us spend years *talking* about doing.'

Others sent checks when Yvonne told about the Kibera School. Enough money was available to feed the children breakfast. Every morning, it consisted of warm porridge, bread and groundnuts. Twice a week, they were given fruit. For many of them, it was their only meal for the day. Of fifty children that enrolled, we were able to acquire sponsorship for 35, and more sponsors were coming on board.

On days when one of the teachers and I canvassed the area to talk to mothers regarding educational sponsorship, I learned that many of them thought education was wasted on girls. They said that sons should be sent to school because girls needed only to marry.

One mothers explained what she saw as the only importance for having girls.

She said, "In order to get dowry, my sister gave her eleven-year-old daughter to a man 44 years old because he had promised to feed her properly—the girl was benefited."

Graduation plans had to be made, but when I discussed the matter with Pastor Charles, he appeared to be wary of having such an event. He said that all public meetings (over 5 people) required a permit from the government. It sounded like a simple matter. Charles favored a graduation, but acted reluctant to take me into town to get the permit.

In behalf of the children, there were times I had to be bold; other times, certain circumstances arose when an inferior demeanor or a subservient countenance worked best. Yet, there were times when neither was effective, as on the day that I waited for two hours, before being ushered into the office of a sarcastic government minister.

He sucked his teeth and said, "Madam, you're asking for a permit to do *what?*"

"Honorable Odhiambo," I began, "thank you very much for seeing me and sorry to take your precious time. We wish to give a graduation for poor children of Kibera."

"Here in Kenya," he curtly explained, "graduation is something we have at university levels. Kenyans do not waste money on unimportant things, like you Americans do. You people are so rich that you use money on frivolous things." After sucking his teeth, he added, "I can't allow you to hold such a public meeting and waste time and mon-ney."

I curbed my resentment and said, "But pleezee, Sir, it's just to recognize the teachers' efforts and to encourage the children. I will finance it if..."

"My answer is 'no' Madam, in fact, I-I can't imagine that I'm *actually* trying to reason with a wom-mon, an American Nee-gro, of all things." With disgust, he waved his hand in a dismissing motion, as one would a pest.

Any ideas I may have had that this would be a smooth-sailing assignment were soon dispelled. I left the office with the realization that *'one who bears a cross does not leap, but trudges along step by step.'*

Without a permit, there could be no graduation; although disappointed, I continued to prepare. On my six-month anniversary in Kenya, I was buried under powder blue fabric, and trying to measure it for caps and robes, then sewed them with needle and thread. The good part about it was that same sizes would fit most of the 22 graduates.

Next, it was back to my writing, and I had begun to write a newsletter to send to family and sponsors. Also I recalled that many newspapers in the United States printed community news free of charge, as a public service. With that in mind, I typed and sent announcements to two of the daily newspapers. A request was made for the event to be covered by one of their reporters, to show the importance of the children's graduation.

From experience, I had seen that politicians covet publicity; therefore, I wrote a letter to invite President Moi to be our Graduation Guest of Honor—or send a representative. Of course, the President of Kenya was not coming to the slums, but I held hope that he may send the tea-maker from his office.

On weekends, I tried to catch up on writing to family and friends; I wrote to my friend Kathy who lived in St. Louis. We had worked together when she was secretary in the Lt. Governor's Office, but she had taken another job before I left for Kenya.

In my letter, I asked Kathy to see if her new boss would give a donation to the children from his shoe company; although solicitation is not allowed. A note added: 'be certain to tell him that I can't afford to even pay for the postage.'

Meanwhile, I had also asked Valerie about the possibility of free printing of public notices in Kenya. She offered some welcomed news.

"I don't know about such things," she said, "but my brother Njoroge is a journalist, and he can tell you how they do things. If I can ever catch him at home, I'll arrange for you two to meet and talk."

3. AS I SAT WHERE THEY SAT

Whether foreign or domestic, we come to recognize that day-to-day discomforts and disappointments are built into the fabric of mission work. Without discrimination, I became baptized in the reality of daily life in Africa. Before long, my knuckles were skinned and sore from washing clothes by hand, on an old-time scrub board in a tin-tub filled with water.

Never before had I used such primitive methods, although as a child, I had learned from my mother how to hang clothes on a line with clothespins. Rationed electric altered my lifestyle and daily functions. If electric was off in our area in A.M., then we ironed at night; when running water was off for four days, we stored up water in jugs. Many areas had no taps for running water.

Women and children walked long distances, stood in lines—20 deep—to buy water in big cans or jugs, and take it home. Unfortunately, a tiny child could spill most water from a heavy can before arriving home.

Kenyans became frustrated over shortages in the stores of sugar, flour, rice, and sometimes milk. Along with 75 others, I had stood in a line that formed as early as 5:00 a.m., at the Uchumi supermarket waiting for the store to open at 8 a.m. to buy one kilo of sugar. Our biggest risk: the sugar might sell out before we could reach the stack, for several weeks the shelves could be empty.

The absence of commodities in the supermarkets was viewed as more corruption of the Moi Regime, and gave credence to the suspicion that food was being used for bribes to gain favorable votes in the coming election.

Kenyan friends believed that under their one-party system, members of KANU behaved as if they were above the government, Judiciary and the Parliament. As such, KANU spurned existing laws in Kenya and made up laws, as they deemed necessary.

Tenacious politicians in KANU practiced an iron-fisted, but shrouded, policy of divide and rule. Throughout Nairobi and surrounding areas, tribal clashes and growing dissension between KANU and rising opposition leaders threw the country into chaos.

With this volatile atmosphere, the president declared a State of Emergency, and it prevented me from going to collect my mail, or move about in the country. Educators, clergymen and lawyers openly called for drastic changes in the country and made attempts at peaceful protest, but their efforts were thwarted by KANU. Some university students rioted, turned over buses, looted and set fires in market places.

The police made arrests, but did not allow legal representation for detainees and would not release any information as to where they were being held. Allegedly, some were tortured. Families appealed for 'due process of the law' in behalf of detainees.

One day, a group of mothers held a prayer vigil in Uhuru Park, praying that Moi would either release their sons or allow legal counsel, and to have contact with family.

Without warning, a large troop of Police Special Units arrived at the park with their automatic rifles then turned water from fire hoses on the unarmed praying mothers, in order to disperse them and to make the women fearful to speak out.

The rest of us did the best we could with what we had. Tests were ongoing, but I continued my measuring and sewing; tassels had to be secured enough on the caps to withstand rough handling from little curious hands.

Much later, dealing with cultural shock, ethnic differences, rejection and political restraints I began to whine to God that some people had an ungrateful attitude toward me. So one rainy Sunday morning, when I was the speaker and waded my way to the church in mud/slush strong enough to pull off a boot and strong winds had turned my umbrella inside out, it was then that God addressed my complaints.

He said, **"Out of millions of Kenyans, not one of them asked ME for you; be glad that you're counted worthy to tread mud to take the gospel."**

This felt like a sharp rap across the knuckles. It truly takes a loving God to inoculate us against diseases that wars against the soul, like 'murmuring and complaining.' It served to help me to see people of Kibera as more of a blessing to me than I was to them.

At the church, I looked for opportunities to show the women their value because most of them had little, if any, self-esteem. Women Auxiliaries or special days for women to use their talents, or to be shown appreciation did not exist, so I arranged to have a Mother's Day celebration at Pastor Charles' church.

I made paper flowers into corsages, bought cookies and cakes, then asked the pastor to provide free sodas. At church, the men did not object, after I explained that God watches how kindly the sisters are treated.

"Since I arrived in this country," I said, "it's only women who always served the tea; on Mother's Day Sunday no female should lift a serving tray." To the men's surprise I added, "Each brother has to pin a flower on a sister near him, shake her hand and serve her refreshments as you say 'God bless you.'"

The brothers were full of smiles and were cooperative, but frowns came when one of the sisters asked, "Can we do this again next Sunday?"

When church service ended, a few teenagers gathered around me, and they had an unusual request. It was a heartfelt concern to them, and I was not hesitant to give them a sincere promise.

One teen asked, "Sustah Maggie, will you tell American youth that we wear clothes; we do not go naked, and African girls do wear bras."

Another commented, "Our garments may not have the style as those worn by Americans, but we're properly dressed, at all times. Your media has portrayed us as wild and running naked through a jungle in need of rescue by a white man named Tarzan. Let them come and see that we're intelligent people and NOT heathens."

Another young minister, in his early thirties said, "I need your prayers and advice on how to get a wife because it is difficult to find the woman of my choice."

"Minister Joshua," I asked, "what kind of woman are you looking for?"

"Ohoo, not too tall, healthy, but not fat, and she must be brown, not very dark."

"Brown–why do you say that she has to be brown?" What is wrong with a sister who is very dark?" I said.

He said, "But, Sustah Maggie, the elders at home in the rural areas tell us not to get a dark woman, if I do, she will give me 'black' children and it is easier to ask for more dowry when your daughter is brown."

"Such a thing is *not* the most important for a good marriage. It's whether you can get along together, be kind, respect one another, and both of you love the Lord; not her color. I can see that you're sincere about this," I stated.

Joshua laughed and said, "In the world we live in, not even Africans want 'black' babies. Maybe if a child is not dark, possibly, they can find happiness before they die—I want my children to have a future; otherwise... I just don't know."

Meanwhile, what would have been considered my quiet time, two incidents happened that awakened my spirit to confrontations with the 'unseen' and I called them Spirit alerts. The first came in a disguised form.

A gray and white, medium size cat made its favorite hangout in the tall grass just below my bedroom window. Sounds from the cat were nothing like the meows usually expected from a feline, or mating cries. Rather, at various times, it made cries like a baby, roars like cubs, howls and grunts like other small animals.

As a Christian, I believed that I should have peaceful sleep and not be disturbed by a demonic cat. For two nights, I prayed about the problem. On the third night, the roars began as I said my prayers; I decided it was time for *action* and I got off my knees.

Time had come to show the little animal that I was in charge. Of course, I had seen on TV and heard how such things should be handled, so I boldly walked to the open window, looked out at the cat and rebuked it—in Jesus Name!

This cat **did not** dash away, as I expected and *hoped*; instead, with split-second precision, it sprang upon the windowsill, back bristled up, and looked directly into my eyes. Startled! I held my breath, jumped back from the window, and ran for the door.

As I reached for the doorknob, the Holy Spirit said to me: **"Greater is He that is in you than he that is in the cat."** I abruptly stopped, returned to the window and, this time, I handled it differently with a simple prayer request.

"Lord, I ask You to silence this cat's tongue so it can no longer disturb my sleep and peace."

The cat scatted away, and did not interfere again with my rest. Two days later, Barbara said, "That old cat must be gone that kept up so much noise."

I smiled, hunched my shoulders, and went out to hang clothes on the line. In the yard crouched in grass, the cat looked at me and opened its mouth several times in a meow gesture. When no sound could be heard, I remembered the prayer for its silence, and in my heart I gave thanks to God.

On the heels of the cat incident, I learned the hard way that a certain tribe in Kenya mourned their dead for a whole week, longer, if the body had been embalmed. In my opinion, that may not be strange in itself, but their manner of grieving for the dead presented a problem.

In a neighborhood not far from Barbara, a family lost a loved one in an accident; the box with the body set in their sitting room. A parade of men, women and children came to show their love for the deceased, day by day; conceivably, the loudest and longest screams revealed the relative with the greatest love. Anyone that appeared to silently grieve drew insolent stares.

It amounted to a contest as to who loved the deceased person the most. About 5:00 each morning, the loud grieving would begin. At first, I thought it was a husband beating his wife, and also considered that someone had suddenly received bad news.

By continuing the third day through 9:30 p.m., I could not imagine what the problem was or why the police were not called. I asked Barbara and she explained that it was a tribal custom.

"I think it's those Luyahs. Some of these tribes carry on like that anytime one dies, and nobody bother them because it is their tradition." She added, "Not even the police do anything to interfere with them—it can be a nuisance."

I felt helpless, but as the fourth-day mourning began, the Holy Spirit told me what to do. I put on my robe and house slippers, eased out of the door, and walked to a short distance but stood visible in clear view from the house of the bereaved. With my arms folded across my breast, I stood motionless.

Mourners who milled around in the yard could clearly see me. An unbroken line of screamers marched into the door, then two or three others would exit the house in a second-breath wail.

When people in the yard began to notice, they pointed me out to others. One woman, whose mouth was wide open, cut her yell short when she looked across at me. With her mouth still open, she, too, stood silent in a momentary gaze then they began to murmur among themselves.

As others looked toward me, the yard was hushed, except for a few sounds inside the house. Within ten minutes, I walked back home, eased into our door, and later, shared with Barbara what had happened.

"Lord! Sister Maggie," she said, "they might have thought you were somebody who had come back from the dead, and it scared the *daylights* out of 'em."

I replied, "Well, I was probably looking bad enough..."

"No, I mean the Holy Spirit put a look on your face that shook 'em up."

Occasionally, Barbara and I teamed with Pastor Juma and other preachers to participate in weekend open-air services in the rural areas. Pastor Paul supported his wife and seven children by teaching school, and this gave him knowledge of when a boarding school auditorium would be available for use.

We took turns to bring a lesson through the afternoons and early evenings, in order to be finished before it was dark, and electricity was not available in the bush. It was marvelous to see thousands come to the open-air services; they climbed up in trees and sat on fences and balconies.

We saw many people respond to an Invitation to Christ with weeping and brokenness; morning services led into afternoons. The moon in Kenya appeared to hang low–within arms' reach so we walk by moonlight. Although I stepped high and wide, my feet would invariably find a puddle of mud or a pothole; I was used to streetlights. Not one Kenyan stumbled, or stepped into a puddle on the rough roads.

Always, when the message and altar prayer was finished, the elders would begin to beat big drums then men, women and children began to dance. It was a lovely sight to see all of them joined with us in giving praise.

The differences between the group of preachers with whom Barbara worked and the licensed preachers in AC served as an advantage for me. Pastor Paul and his group were those *that heard the call to go into the vineyard,* obtained certificates but not formal training. They took us to grass root Kenyans, in areas where there were few churches.

The bishop of AC told me, "All our ministers are seminary graduates, but the Assembly of God did not approve of giving pastoral credentials to men that were divorced or believed in having a second wife. In our culture, a young man could have a *traditional marriage* and to simply pay the dowry then take the girl as his bride, long before he was in a position to attend the seminary."

I asked, "So coming to Nairobi made a difference?"

"You see," the bishop continued, "once they left home to get educated in Nairobi, it was not unusual for a man to meet another woman, get a Certificate of Marriage and have a proper church wedding. In our view, as we come into the light, we took proper steps to walk in it. We recognized that it was strictly cultural differences, therefore, we organized the Assemblies of Christ to embrace alienated seminary graduates."

4. MAKING HISTORY

"Show me thy ways, O Lord; teach me thy paths." Psalm 25:4 (AJKV)

Pastor Charles' wife Valerie was faithful to her word. One Saturday morning, she picked me up in her Volkswagen, and told me that her brother would talk to me about how to put a notice in the newspaper. In keeping with Kenya custom, Valerie made a quick stop to purchase milk, bread, margarine and a dozen eggs.

Gloria, Valerie's sister-in-law, greeted us at the door and received the groceries. After introductions, Gloria went to get her husband. As Njoroge approached me to shake hands, Valerie reminded him of why we had come.

He began, "Now, just let me try to understand this. God, Himself, spoke and told you to come to Nairobi, and now He says for you to give a graduation to nursery school children—even though, God knows this is not a custom in Kenya. I think you also sent a request letter to the <u>Daily Nation</u> about this matter. Is that right?"

"Wel-ll, yes." I tried to explain, "When God first told me to come, I had no idea what I was coming to do in Nairobi... so I'm taking this a day at a time."

The 34-year old father began to trace my features with his small bug-eyes, in search of pretense, confusion or to determine if he should seriously trust the alien seated in front of him. My motives for being in his country were highly questionable to the journalist.

He said, "This is very interesting. I-I don't believe I've ever *met* anybod-dy who said they actually had dialogue with God." With a deep-thought furrow across his brow, he added, "What is that like—thunder? A noise?" he probed, "A feeling? Or ju-just what *does* God's voice sound like?"

I suspected that his interest had now turned to mockery; I had no patience or desire to waste his time or mine. If he could not offer significant help then I would look elsewhere, to not disappoint the children.

I looked directly in his face and said, "Njoroge, I suppose that every person communicates with God the way he chooses; I'm not a fool or a religious fanatic."

I continued, "This is definitely not an assignment I asked for, but God proved to me that I had no options but to come here. Somehow, there'll be a graduation, although the government refused to give me a permit."

He shuffled in his chair, "Please, p-please, don't get me wrong," his tone was apologetic, "I think it's a fine thing you're doing. You know, it's just strange to talk to one who claims to hear God's voice... like... M-Moses, you know—has God's ear."

Valerie came to my rescue, "Then will you see if your paper will print an announcement for her, and how much it will cost?"

"Let me talk to my editor," he said to her and glanced back at me, "I'll contact you through my sister. Probably, we can do something but I don't know what."

Forty-year-old Valerie felt confident that her brother would assist her in any way. She had helped to pay for his education, and over the years, she never missed a chance to remind him, if she needed a favor. As for me, I knew the matter was in God's hands.

As purpose dictated, I designed certificates to present in categories of Attendance, Class Status, and merit awards for the teachers. Also, I sent a request to my daughter Yvonne for a box of gold seals so that they could be put on graduation certificates.

At times of loneliness and missing my family, usually, a song or prayer would pull me through it. But one day, I felt as if I could not bear to spend another week without my daughters; my longing for them brought flowing tears.

The Holy Spirit said: ***If you allow yourself to become emotionally paralyzed, then I can not use you effectively here.***

Thereafter, I stayed focused on my work and began to think of myself as being at home, in Kenya—with no place else to go. The children of Kibera needed two things God had given to me: a mother's heart and a worker's spirit. As precious as those *lambs* were in God's sight, I prayed to do the job in a way to put a smile on the Good Shepherd's face. I knew His will; my part was to obey.

On Madaraka Day (June 1st), Pastor Charles brought a notice that gave me overwhelming joy. The Claim Notice indicated that a box came to the airport, mailed from Taiwan, with shipping and handling paid. Kathy's boss sent shoes and paid for the handling out of his pocket. One hundred pairs of shoes sent in various sizes, in individual plastic bags. I thought, we had to only go to the airport and get them.

"So, Pastor," I said, "to collect the shoes we just go to the airport, show proper credentials and get the box from Cargo Import?"

"No-oo, that might not be a good idea; it's best to go early next week. I am sure it will take some time. No business transaction was a simple process in Kenya."

I could not understand why Pastor insisted that we would wait out the weekend then go to the airport on Monday. I had many lessons to learn about how things were done in Kenya.

That Friday, Gloria came to say that her husband wanted me to meet him in town, at the New Stanley Hotel for lunch. At first, panic swept over me, but I held some hope that his boss had approved an inexpensive way for the newspaper to assist us.

On Friday, I left school and headed for the bus stop it was slower but safer to catch the KBS, although the bus might have an unfastened long, rear window that flopped and banged for the entire route, over trenches and potholes. Passengers standing on the bus had, literally, breathing space only.

On the bus floor could be three or four live chickens tied together, or a four-foot sack of potatoes or onions. Larger sacks were on top of the bus, where bed mattresses were transported. The alternative was to ride with reckless drivers in matatus (minibuses) that caused multiple collisions, turnovers and deaths. In a crammed over capacity matatu, it was not unusual to find a stranger leaned on your lap or across your shoulders.

I found Njoroge in the Patio Restaurant of the hotel. I was not in the mood for any *jokes,* but after we placed our lunch order, Njoroge started by telling the result of the talk with the Daily Nation Editor.

"Uh huh, so I've discussed the matter about the graduation with my boss, and he says I can put something together for his approval. About the permit, maybe we can also find somebody who has the president's ear," he said.

My countenance softened and I smiled, "I'm grateful for whatever you'll do."

"Then just relax, Maggie," he said.

"Njoroge, my interest lies in getting help for these children, and I'm happy that you're willing to help us. Kenyan women work hard to eke something out of nothing; it ages them beyond their years, and they're robbed of their youth and beauty. Anything I can possibly do to lighten their load, I will try it. I know God loves Kenya."

"Do you know that here in Kenya, we called the Mamas, *beast of burdens?"* he said and ordered another Coke Cola.

His next question caught me off guard. "Can you tell me how this conversation with God began?" He added, "I mean, how did this all come about?"

With a deep sigh and effort, I attempted to give him the story in a capsule form: how it initially began with our family prayer, on Saturdays in St. Louis; I dragged my feet for two years, and the God-given assurances that I had received.

He listened, and looked with squint eyes into my face with a 'don't miss anything' *journalist expression,* and he let me talk uninterrupted about five minutes. For a moment, he seemed without words and gave a quick nervous smile, as I finished.

He said, "Is it like... I mean, will God tell you about sin in a person's life?"

"Usually, it's the misbehavior in my own life that He addresses. No, I'm not a psychic—the motive and intent of your heart is God's business—not mine."

"Wel-ll, that's very good," he looked relieved and said, "maybe I'll talk more about it another time. But could you arrange one day

AN EAR TO HEAR

for me to go to school with you, and to take pictures of you with the kids—maybe photograph one trying on a robe?"

"Sure, just call me when you're ready. Monday, I'm going to the airport because an international shoe company based in the States has donated 100 pairs of shoes for the children at the school. It's so exciting what God is doing in Kibera."

On Monday morning, Pastor Charles came early. I made certain to have my passport and Work Permit, and reminded myself to do nothing to cause a Kenyan official to interpret as *American arrogance*.

The rules were set. At the airport, Charles and I found the Cargo storage area and presented my Postal Claim to the attendant, but I kept the credentials in my hand.

"We would like to get this package," I said to the clerk.

Once he looked at the claim, he motioned me to wait; forty-five minutes later, a box was set on the counter for me to open in front of airport personnel. The clerk briefly looked in the box then went into a small office; more waiting.

Since shipping and handling were paid and I had proper I.D., it was difficult to see why we could not leave with the box. Charles made no comments at all, with his head lowered for the whole time and his eyes were down cast.

Finally, a supervisor came up to the counter, with a strictly business approach, and gave meticulous examination of the box for about 30 seconds. He looked point blank into my eyes and said that he could not release the shoes.

"In fact," he asserted, "we are to burn such things brought into this country, according to the Kenya laws."

"Burn! B-but I have identification—the box is addressed to me." When he would not relent, I asked, "Who's in charge? We must talk to someone else."

Charles and I were directed to the third floor office of the Minister of Imports/Exports. We climbed the stairs and waited a half an hour to see the minister, and his reply was not surprising.

He took the claim form, sat up and leaned elbows on his huge desk then looked at us in a half smile. He appeared to enjoy this part of his job.

"Madame," he said, "unfortunately, people come here and do not bother to become knowledgeable about the Kenya Government's laws." He glanced at the claim again, "Now in this case, it would not be in the best interest of Kenya manufacturers, if we let shoes come into this country. It would undermine our economy; Kenyans also make shoes to sell. Better for you to have asked for the mon-ney and buy here."

In reply I said, "Honorable Minister, the shoes are donated to children in Kibera, no Kenya manufacturer will do that. We plan to give the shoes away; not sell them."

"It is not in my power to give them to you; we are under strict orders from the president himself. Perhaps you are qualified to get a wavier in town, until then, the shoes will remain at the airport," the government minister said.

Charles and I left in a hurry to go into town. The situation was not much different at the Wavier/Special Permit Office, and it soon became obvious that only bribery would spur any consideration given to us. After the officer told stories about how *"utterly impossible"* it was to obtain such a wavier, I asked Charles to take me home.

"If you'll take me where I can get on my knees, we'll get those shoes and not pay one shilling for them," I said, "The Shepherd will not send His lambs shoes and let the laws of man take them away. Tomorrow, those shoes will be released."

That night I prayed; none of this had taken God by surprise, and He gave me a way to handle it. The next morning, we went to the Social Service Division and I explained to them my dilemma. My Work Permit had been issued through the Minister of Social Service, and he had authority over my actions in the country.

In 20 minutes, the Minister of Social Services gave me an envelope sealed with wax. Then he said that if the shoes were not released, I should telephone him, before leaving the airport. Back at the Import/Export Office, the minister in charge bristled; his motion was laborious when he stamped Release Approved on my claim slip.

Charles and I hurriedly took the box of shoes and once we were safely in the car; we laughed and repeatedly emphasized the story about the look of defeat on the minister's face. Not one shilling was paid in bribes.

I laughed and said, "Yeah! I don't know what was written in the Social Service letter, but that minister sure looked beaten," bursting with victory I added, "He dreaded to put 'release' on the papers," I demonstrated how the minister banged the stamp down.

"Me?" Charles finally found his voice, "I was too scared to breathe. See, you don't know these people in Kenya like I do. They can be very treacherous." With an after thought he said, "I can tell you, those shoes would not have been burned but sold on the street, so someone in parliament could get the money and buy plenty of yuma choma (roasted meat) for themselves. Aaye!! God is good."

With that hole punched in the devil's defeat bag, I could not forget the manager responsible for sending the shoes. In prayer that night, I felt led to send the manager this message from God: **Not only does God heal diseases, but He also heals relationships**.

There were no shortages in tests that continued to come. Inadvertently, I learned that Barbara intended to move out of the house and that she had passed the word on to her friends and neighbors.

It came to my attention when she had gone to spend a three-day weekend with a friend. I seized the chance to meditate and pray as I shampooed my hair. No sooner than I had rolled my hair on curlers, a woman came to the door and asked for Barbara Jones.

Although she was not sure if she had the right house, she was quite definite about the person that she wanted to find.

I said, "I am sorry, Sister Jones is not here, but this is where she lives."

"Well, my name is Rachel. Someone told me to come and tell this Sustah Jones about a very nice house that's vacant, and I've come to take her to see it."

Still, I believed that the woman was in the wrong place. Early on, Barbara had taught me to always offer (at least) tea and biscuits (cookies) when a Kenyan comes to the house because you never know how far they have had to travel, on foot.

"My name is Maggie; I will make some tea and you may come in, write a note for Sister Jones, and I'll be happy to give it to her when she returns on Monday," I suggested.

"No-oo," Rachel said, stepping inside the door, "the person who owns the house needs to know today, if Sustah Barbara wants to rent the place."

"You just have a seat, while I fix tea. All I can think is that it's a mistake.

Maybe... you're looking for another Barbara."

The short, small-boned woman looked to be in middle forties, had a gap in her front teeth, without any makeup and her face looked peaceful. Her neatly fitted blouse had a matching skirt that hung below her knees; a spotless white scarf covered her head.

She was a school teacher, her husband a banker, and they had two sons in collage, two other boys and a girl in secondary school. With her humble, unpretentious manner, I felt drawn to this lady; Rachel was someone easy to like. However, she was persistent. Over the years, I considered myself to be very persuasive, but in Rachel, I met my match.

She said, "My Sustah is there a phone where I may reach this Sustah Barbara?"

"No, there is no way to reach her, and I don't think she wants to move out of this house, until she permanently leaves for the States." I continued, "We share expenses of this house, and she's said nothing about our giving up this place. That's the reason I think you have confused her with someone else."

"I am verr-ry sure," Rachel stressed, "because this house was pointed out and they said it was a Black American missionary who lived here and wanted to move out."

Then she added, "This place I'm talking about has never been rented before now, it was just built. I know that God has it for somebody... maybe Sustah Jones."

I offered to give Barbara the note Rachel had written, but it did not help. She held on doggedly; although I had grown impatient, I had to admire her determination.

"My Sustah," she urged, "why can't you come with me to see the house so you can tell her how it looks? It's two rooms with a small kitchen and indoor shower."

Rachel was like a dull toothache; not unbearable, but would not go away. I tried to explain that Barbara's large furniture may not fit in a small place. Further, I said that my hair was wet and I could not go out in hair rollers. However, Rachel had an answer.

"But can't you put on a headscarf? We're not going far—*it's just here*," she pointed west and said, "I'll take you there and bring you back after you have seen it."

Finally, I agreed to join her, and we walked for six long blocks, before we arrived at the Harambee Estates. The landlord was Rachel's friend and fellow-teacher, whose husband (a big man in the police department) built servant-quarters in back of their main house, and left it to his wife to find a suitable tenant.

Eve Atenio was almost as tall as I, and wore her medium length hair combed back with no curls. Although she was Catholic, and Rachel was Christian, they had maintained close contact for several years. With practiced subservience, Eve kept a low tone in her heavy voice and her eyes stayed downcast when she spoke.

"If Jones can't use the house, why don't you take it?" She asked, "How much furniture do you have?"

I laughed and said, "Not any, not even a bed of my own—my finances are small. Anyway, how much will you charge for rent? I've heard that Kenyan landlords raise the rent regularly, without notice."

Eve quickly said, "If you want it, is 2000/shillings (about $115) acceptable?"

I told her that the monthly amount was reasonable, but we needed to see how Sister Jones would decide. She deserved to see it for herself, and I could not possibly take it before then, or speak in her behalf.

"I wasn't holding the house for that lady—I've never met her." Eve said, "I just want the right tenant because I have four children, and my husband cautioned me to be careful who moves in here. So if Jones leaves, won't you also need a place to live? It has a full-sized bed in there already."

"Oh, yes I could gradually get some furniture pieces–we shall see. One thing for sure, the next time a Kenyan tells me that a place is *'just here'* I will pack a lunch and change of clothes."

We had a laugh about it. Then Rachel and I left with the understanding that if Barbara did not take the place, then I would rent it. As we reached the Buru Buru Estates, I felt fatigue in mind and body, and perplexed about Barbara's silence. As I approached the yard, I noticed a man and woman at the door. They introduced themselves as Barbara's landlords, Jacob and Jacqueline, and they had come to see Barbara about a rent check.

Jacob said, "We had heard that you were here to help Barbara—we are glad because she needs plenty help so she can stop giving me those bad checks."

"I'm not sure what you mean." I said, "Because I give her my half in cash, so…"

The young couple explained that for the past three years, Barbara had had some money problems, and at least half of the time, she would have insufficient funds for her rent check. Jacob speculated that I may have given cash, but when Barbara wrote a check for the full amount, her half was not in the bank.

Jacqueline made no comment, until she said, "She has told us about your work in Kibera, and that you're helping those poor children. I'm a supervisor at the general hospital, and if any one of the kids gets sick bring them in, and ask for me. Maybe I can get cheaper medicine with my discount or do something else to help you."

On our way to church on Sunday morning, I learned that Pastor Charles and Valerie knew nothing of Barbara's wish to vacate the house. I kept reminding myself that God knows where He wants me, even if another door had to be opened.

About 8:00 p.m., Barbara returned home with uplifting testimonies of how God healed as she ministered, and she had thoroughly enjoyed her weekend. She made no mention of plans to move, however, she did ask if anyone had come to visit her.

I said, "The landlord and his wife came by. He had a question about the rent check, and said that you'll have to get a money order from now on."

"That money was in the bank, but my account is not straightened out yet from what somebody took without my approval." Ruefully she added, "I wouldn't give anyone a bad check."

After a two-minute silence, I took a deep breath and said, "Another lady came by to tell you about a house; someone told her that you were interested in moving—I had no idea what she meant."

"Yeah, I'm fleecing the Lord because I'm tired of trying to get Jacob to fix things, and he lies about getting my rent on time. So I asked some friends to help me to find somewhere else to live," she said, "I can't keep on putting up with that devil –Jacob."

"I'm sorry that you didn't tell me how you felt," I said with effort to remain calm. "Barbara, I could not afford this house alone, any more than you can."

With a pensive expression, she said that things were not going right for her, and it might be God letting her know that it was time to pack up and go back home to stay.

Finally I said, "I have seen the house; there're two medium size rooms, and a small kitchen and you should see it just in case you will be interested. Mrs. Atenio has offered it to me, but not until we see what you think or your decision about it."

"Nooo, child, I've got too much stuff for that little space. I would hate to see you go, but if you do, may God bless ya. My friend who lives on Valley Road asked me to move in with her, until I decide. Of course, I don't do anything unless I fleece the Lord first, to see if it is His will."

For the rest of March, I packed up my things; cleaned my bedroom and scrubbed down the shower room. While I mopped the floor, a 2500/shillings figure was impressed on my mind, as I meditated on the decision to move away.

By 9:00 a.m. April 1, Mr. & Mrs. Atenio came in their truck to assist me to move. At the new house, I handed Eve the first month's rent.

"Oh!" she said, "You've given me too much, remember, we agreed 2000/."

"Yes, but the Lord wants me to pay 2500/, so that's what I have to do."

She said that it was the first time she heard of a tenant raising the rent. I simply explained that since God has raised my rent, it indicates that He is going to increase my finances. Already, He had given me a place never before occupied.

The bedroom was about the size of the one at Barbara's, but I had a double bed and a small plastic table nearby. In the 4'x 4' shower room, the toilet bowl was (for some strange reason) situated down in a hole, so the commode top was even with the floor; the flush tank was extended off the floor by four feet of plastic pipe.

Since 50th - year was close enough to wipe the hot-flash sweat off my brow I discovered my newest challenge in the toilet was to get up from a squatting position. By the time I rallied my zeal, it could cause me to forget why I went to the toilet, in the first place. A tight race could have been waged between what I needed most: 3-in-1 oil, 10W-40 or vitamin B-12 *concentrate*. Never thought the day would come when I could have appreciated that a bathroom had no mirrors.

Harambee Estates was considered as one of the more affluent areas in which to live, at least, for my purposes, it was nearer to the bus stop. One day, Mr. Atenio noticed the constant gaze that his children gave me, and he explained why they did it.

"The children are trying to determine your tribe." He said, "Actually, you could be Somali or Ethiopian with your skin color, also, Maasai women are slim and tall, but actually, no Kenyan woman is as tall as you."

In addition, he told of various traditions (depending on the tribe): the men pull out three front, bottom teeth; another, mostly Kikuyu and Maasai pierced their earlobes. As the hole grew, bigger items would be pressed into the hole, until the earlobe hung down.

Within first two weeks in Harambee, a commotion started in the neighborhood, but the high bricked walls that surrounded the compound prevented me from seeing. So I walked up to the front gate, stood beside the Atenio's house girl and peeped out.

Just as I looked through the gate, a huge dog ran passed in high speed; it was being chased by a group of young kids. They yelled, waved a stick and romped through the neighborhood after it, until the end of the lunch time and they returned to school.

The next day, my hair-raising chill came as we learned from the media and newspapers that it was not a dog, but a LION. The animal had gotten loose while being transported in back of a truck to one of the national parks.

† † † † †

A surprising message came in a letter from my friend Kathy in St. Louis. She wrote that her manager/boss who sent me the shoes told of a personal problem he had. *'His marriage was weakening under the pressure of a long distant relationship. She worked in Los Angeles; he in St. Louis, and neither of them wanted to leave their jobs. The very day that he received your letter, the shoe company had notified him that two positions were opened in another state. If he and his wife agreed on the salary, they could make immediate plans to move, and he was happy to say that the transition would save their marriage.'*

With a reputation of 'always' being late, Njoroge was punctual the day he accompanied me to the school. As we headed to the bus stop for a 45-minute ride to Kibera, I wondered if he had any idea what he would face. He chose to travel the exact way that I used each morning, and he appeared undaunted by the path.

He said, "You know, most foreigners come and stay in the more modern and convenient houses, but you live here as Kenyans live; I think that's also how your Peace Corps do it. Americans do good work when they leave US riches to come to places like Kibera and help. Also, I think that's why you Americans are so blessed."

"With me," I replied, "it is not how righteous I am or even that I'm so qualified, but I believe God *causes* some things which take us beyond our normal capabilities. This is one of those."

We stepped off the bus at the station in Kibera, and began the walk through the overgrown bushy hill to the railroad. Once we had crossed the tracks, there was another kilometer to get to the school. Along the way, Njoroge spoke about the conditions.

"I can't imagine that you actually trek through all this stuff every day. I wonder if it is worse in the dust during hot months, or to walk on slippery mud in long rains." He said while trying to shake mud off his tennis shoes.

Children played in mud puddles with toys made of sticks and wire. Down at the Kibera River, mothers washed family laundry with homemade soap. Four or five toddlers stood lined on the side of the path, ready to give me their daily morning greeting.

"Habari! Black Mzungu (Mzungu: an English speaking person), habari," they began in unison as I walked pass them. Their morning singsong greeting continued until I was out of sight. They heartedly laughed when I returned their greeting in kind.

At the school, our 50 children pushed to get a turn to shake my hand, by then, I had learned to look beyond their soiled hands, urine-smelling clothes and tear-streaked faces and swarming flies. Headmistress is all they knew; no significance to them that I had previously worked in an office with carpeted floors or had been seen on television.

Inside, I called to one of the prospective graduates and tried on a robe to mark the hem guides. Njoroge wrote notes and took pictures of the school and my interacting with the children then he left and went back to town.

Later, I went to the post office and found mail from the Office of the President. The envelope was sealed on back with wax, only to notify me that the president would be out of the country and not available for our event. That part did not surprise me, but no reference was made as to a possible representative coming from his office.

There was no other place, I knew, to find a proper guest to be our speaker. Later in the evening, Gloria (Njoroge's wife) came to visit, and it was good to get better acquainted with her. She told me that Njoroge used to be a church member but had gotten out of church, and not gone back for the past three years. She was a kindhearted young lady and willing to give help whenever she could.

Gloria also brought me a 13-inch television, which was in her daughter's room and seldom used. It felt very good to know someone in the country, like my landlords and Gloria, cared to check on me as a neighbor, not just for an American.

The following Thursday morning at 7:30, Eve was knocking on the door to get me for a phone call. Hurriedly, I dressed, went to the phone and found it was Njoroge.

"Hello!" I said, "Njoroge... Nzuri... You're kidding me? No, I've not seen the Daily Nation... uh huh... yes... Asante sana. Thanks for all you've done."

Excitement flowed through my veins—the story was out. As I ran back into my house, I saw Pastor Charles coming in the gate carrying newspapers in his hand. He stepped high and spry with pride, his grin could not get wider. He handed me a newspaper and came into the house and sat down with an air of dignity.

'A DREAM SHAPES UP IN KIBERA' was the heading of the Daily Nation newspaper feature story about my work. Every word Njoroge had listened to so intensely, he had written. A picture, flanked by columns, showed one of the children trying on a robe.

Charles said, "You keep that paper, I'm going to buy more, they'll have to give us a permit now. I can't stay because I want to pass around several more newspapers." He could visualize himself as an *honorable government minister.*

God had made Njoroge part of the 'construction crew' for Kibera children. I telephoned him later to express appreciation, and to ask about the cost of such a story because my budget was seriously stretched.

"You know I don't have extra money. So Njoroge what do I owe for all this?"

He said, "There is no cost to you. It is a story we're featuring—news you're giving us to report. It is our job; in fact, it's HISTORY in the making." Then he had more wonderful news to announce.

"The Minister of Technical Training called us at <u>NATION</u> House, after he read the story, and he offered to give the help you need. Now go to his office, Maggie, tell him who you are and see what he's willing to do."

He added, "Oh yeah, my boss has assigned me to cover the graduation, I'll come to take pictures, which will be in our newspaper... oh-oo, probably Tuesday."

"I'm so thankful to you for getting involved in Kibera. It was the will of God for us to meet; now you're a part of the blessings of this mission."

"T-that's OK, there's nothing wrong with it—I wouldn't mind to get blessed, in fact, I could use it... maybe speak in tongues... get a salary increase. Maybe go to the States for more studies," he said.

I sense the presence of his devious expression and sly grin. Sometimes, I could not detect when he was serious or being facetious. For certain, over the months, God had used him in ways that Njoroge, himself, had not recognized.

The next day, I went to talk with the Minister of Technical Training. It turned out to be a totally different encounter than the ones I had had before with other officials. He was cordial and decisive. Not only did the minister provide a permit for the graduation, he had arranged for the Langata Member of Parliament to be our speaker.

When the teachers and I met with the parents of graduates, my excitement was dampened by one of the mothers who had lost confidence in anything that involved the Kenya Government.

"Headmistress," she started, "you found me poor—poverty I know ver-ry well; please don't come to this country making promises that will not be kept." She went on, "Many come here to Kenya as Christians and tell all they will give us by way of support, if we let them take photos and film the way our families live.

"We let them do the filming then they go. We get nothing! Although we are lacking many things in Kenya, Headmistress, one thing is left–**the poor still have feelings**. So why should we now trust what you're tell'en us will happen?"

I replied, "I know what you've said is true. Some do come and deceive but not 'all' just like not all Kenyans are trustworthy. Often, organizations are hindered from giving significant help because of governmental regulations that defeat their efforts.

One of the teachers told the parents that not all Kenyans are truthful especially the politicians, and that many times promises are made just to get votes.

I stated, "What I promise you will take place, Mama Richard, the MP for Kibera will be our guest at the graduation. Parents, all I ask is don't let him see empty chairs when he arrives. We will have special chairs reserved for parents to sit at the front, so don't let your children down by staying home."

Still, a few that had little or no knowledge of English shied away from me. They thought that I was in my late-thirties and had come to their country to find myself a husband. Interviews for the sponsorship program served to improve understanding among the parents, and with me. I told them about my own family, and we exchanged stories of joys and sorrows in raising children.

Pastor Charles did his part to give the school critically needed cement covering. Gloria, the teachers and I decorated the inside of the building as best as could be expected, and put up a huge 'WELCOME TO OUR GRADUATION' sign on the back wall. I used colorful streamers to reserved chairs for parents of the honorees.

As when a U.S. Senator is guest at a function in the home state and other dignitaries in the area are required to be present, so it was with the graduation when the MP came to Kibera. It grew bigger than I could have imagined; standing room only.

November 1989, drivers in specially marked government cars and police vehicles braved the rough road through the valley, and all local officials came to the Kibera Soweto School. The entrance flanked by male and female law enforcers, AC officials and school staff stood in the receiving line to greet Honorable Philip Leakey, Assistant Minister of Technical Training (the only Kenyan Caucasian in Parliament).

Graduates proudly wore robes, caps with tassels, ready to receive their gold sealed certificates. The girls' hair had curls or braids; boys had a fresh haircut; although some wore old shoes, none came barefooted.

All the parents, including previously alienated fathers, came to occupy their reserved seats; gaping residents lined each side of the rough road; children of all ages were amazed and gave a parade wave as the dignitaries passed by.

The MP's twenty-minute speech to men advised, "Let wives take care of the money." He presented certificates to graduates and awards to teachers. Although Honorable Leakey came from a renowned family, before leaving, he expressed to me that he had no regrets about his participation.

He said, "I'm very happy that I came; I don't know when I've enjoyed something so much."

Njoroge was present, along with a reporter from the Standard newspaper. From the beginning to end, the crowd spilled out into the road; Kibera residents were astounded. It appeared that some gained new hope, because something was needed to rebuild their faith in their Kibera Member of Parliament.

There was soft drinks and cake for all. Many parents thanked me and expressed their approval in my leadership at the school—they believed their children had progressed in their studies, since my arrival.

Someone whispered, "Imagine! Headmistress must be an angel sent from God."

A pair of shoes was given to every one of our students. According to what God had said, it was the only graduation some of them ever had, and with His help, the children were given a graduation in grand style. Once God has spoken and made His will known; our role to hear, heed and continue to walk in His will by faith.

"The Lord God hath opened mine ear, and I was not rebellious, neither turned away..." Isaiah 51:5

The following Tuesday, two daily newspapers carried pictures of the group of graduates and speech excerpts from the Guest of Honor. In days, school enrollment pushed over capacity, and more children came whose parents were able to pay fees. In the following weeks, the church membership grew.

5. TRANSFORMING LIVES

More often than not, there appears to be seasons when God transform lives in a dramatic way, outside the physical church setting. The outreach of the Kibera assignment expanded, as God drew more people into that blessing.

Following the graduation, U.S. sponsors continued to get on board. Lisa, a 22-year-old Accountant in New Orleans, sent one of the 'you don't know me' letters with a check for $25, and was assigned to 7-year-old Lillian whose mother was a single parent.

For Lillian's birthday, Lisa mailed some underwear and a life-sized black doll. The day the package arrived, we took it immediately to Lillian. A teenager greeted us at the door, and my interpreter told her that we had come to see Lillian.

In Kiswahili the teen said, "Lillian is in bed with a severe case of Malaria. I'm the Auntee, and I had to come to baby-sit for Lillian and her ten-month-old brother because their mother had been arrested and jailed for stealing food."

As we stepped inside, we found the child burning with fever. So first, we prayed for the child. When Lillian saw the new underwear, there was little reaction, but I began to take wrapping off the doll and Lillian took more interest. We assisted her to sit up in bed and I handed her the doll, as she extended her arms and held them stiffly. At this point, my interpreter suspected the girl believed the doll was a real baby.

She said, "Mum, this girl was probably allowed by the mother to hold her little brother and was cautioned against letting the baby fall. So Lillian thinks the doll is real."

In seconds, Lillian offered to give back the doll. I told the interpreter to explain to her that the sponsor sent a doll for her birthday–so she could play as a *little mum*. When Lillian understood it was a toy and hers to keep, her mouth opened widely in a smile of pleasant surprise. By the time we left, the fever had subsided and Lillian was sitting up.

Later that week, Gloria invited me for tea and to meet one of her sisters. When I arrived, Gloria said that her sister Naomi had a specific reason why she wanted to see me.

"Mum," Gloria began, "my sister asked if you could help a girl who's really in a bad way, but does not live in Kibera. I told her that you go all over Kenya to help the women and children."

"Of course, if I can do anything. Where is this girl?"

"Naomi is going to take you to the place. In fact, my sister should have been here already, but as we say, 'there are no clocks in Kenya' I think you know that by now."

When Gloria's sister arrived a half hour later, I was introduced to Naomi. The house-girl set tea and biscuits (cookies) on the table, and the three of us talked a few minutes before Naomi began her story.

"There's this girl, Anne, who is seriously sick and her husband put her out and ran her back to the mother. Imagine!" She added, "I had just left mass last Sunday, and I saw her on side of the road."

"I don't usually stop for people," Naomi continued, "but she was pregnant and I thought it was her time, so I questioned her about it. She said that she had walked to town to Rhodes Hospital for an injection, tried to go back home and couldn't make it."

"Mum," Gloria explained, "Rhodes treats TB patients. But I have to go to Ya Ya Center, if you have time, Naomi can take you to see this girl and learn her story."

Because the buses are so slow and the matatus are dangerous, I agreed that Naomi and I could walk while we talked. It was about a 30-minute walk from Gloria's house.

Conditions in Umoja slums were not much different from Kibera; still, it was the first time I had seen a house made of cartons. The two of us approached the field where an isolated hut hid the pain and humiliation of a destitute family of six.

Pieces of cardboard tied to tall sticks held by vines formed the one room house; on the top were dried branches, held down by stones and rocks. The structure had one door, no windows. Outside, shaded by the house, a young woman sat on a three-legged stool. At a glance, her rejected countenance and downcast eyes told part of the story.

Naomi said, "I'll have to interpret for you; she is illiterate and speaks only her mother-tongue, Kikuyu. You see, when one doesn't know the national language of Kiswahili, it means that they have not gone to school."

"That's quite all right with me because my Kiswahili is not that good, anyway." I said, "Kikuyu language is not familiar to me at all."

As the introduction began, the mother came out and brought stools for us to sit. In Kenya, American is synonymous with being rich; therefore, it was necessary to explain to Anne how I did my work. Naomi started her role as interpreter.

"Tell her that I am not sure what I can do, but if she will tell me the truth, I will do my best to help, but *American* doesn't mean that I have lots of money."

Anne gave an affirmative nod. I listened closely to Naomi, and interrupted only if clarification was needed. The coughing had already begun by the 23-year-old mother who was pregnant with the third child.

Anne began to relate her story: The husband put her out when she became too ill to continue to cultivate his farm. After a year up-country in his shamba (garden), she had become sick and was given herbal remedies by her mother-in-law. In about six months, Anne's health grew so bad that she had begun to cough up blood.

On that first time, she visited her husband in Nairobi and requested to see a doctor, but he refused and said, "Your duty is to work in the shamba." He warned her *"Don't forget your place."*

Anne returned to cultivating for three more months. Coughing increased, spitting up more blood, and periodically being (as I understood the description) in a comatose state. Anne became fearful that she was going to die so she returned to Nairobi to plead and beg with the husband for permission to see a doctor.

Then the husband simply dismissed her and said, "If you're too sick to work, you're no use to me; go back to yore mama."

Also, he dared Anne to tell anybody about him, if she did, he threatened to torch the mother's carton house. Tears began to flow down her cheeks, as she took a minute to complete a spasm of coughing.

Because Anne was his third wife to get TB, she was afraid that TB would spread to her whole family, if she did not get cured soon. Anne would continue to go to Rhodes twice a month; no money was available for taking a bus, or a matatu that was cheaper.

"Ask her," I said, "will she allow me to write to newspapers about him, if I don't reveal his name? Other unsuspecting young women may not be as lucky as she and get under his spell, if the story is not told."

Anne readily agreed, and said that before she had gotten their clothes packed, a girl was waiting there to marry him. For an instant, I understood why some people get stoned to death in Kenya, especially if it serves to protect the innocent.

In reality, I did not know what to do, but pray for God's guidance; there was a good reason why Anne and I had to meet. My role was to get her story published; caring and loving people would respond in behalf of the children.

Throughout the conversation, the Mother would add some part of her own tragic story. She told how her 12-year-old son—whom she carried tied to her back, was born with a cyst on his spine. At age five, doctors operated on his back and it left him paralyzed from the waist down.

She was particularly saddened by the son-in-law's mistreatment of her daughter, and his cruel promise to throw paraffin on her house and burn it down. The mother cultivated a small garden to feed her family; usually, with the son tied on her back.

In departure, we promised to be in touch, as soon as we had any news. It was a brief silence between Naomi and I, as we walked away, I felt shaken in my spirit over the pitiful situation. With God's grace, a newspaper might accept Anne's story for print.

"Naomi," I said, "please remind me again of how you found her, I want to be sure to write it correctly."

"When I noticed this girl lying over on the ground and that she was pregnant, I would have to assist her, if she was ready to deliver. That's what we women do in Kenya; you have to help."

Naomi said, "Just imagine! She's over eight months pregnant, coughing with TB, and walking about 20 Kilometers to Rhodes, along the dusty roads. She gets regular injections maybe two times a month," she slowly shook her head at the thought of it.

"Is that when Anne told you about the husband?" I asked.

"You see, when she found that I'm also Kikuyu then she told me. Uumph! These Kenyan men... he marries a girl, gives her TB, then work the poor girl to death, or chases her back to her family," she said in disgust.

"Did you offer to find someone to help them?"

"Of course no, I had bought them bread, milk and eggs before leaving their place but after I got back home and kept thinking about this terrible thing, I felt something else had to be done." The 34-year-old mother continued, "Since I had only seen you at the graduation and in the newspapers, it's my sister who told me the work you do for poor women. I thought you just worked with the children in Kibera.

Naomi glanced at me as she shrugged her shoulders and said, "I was not sure just how to act with you; some Black Americans seem to feel that they are better than we Africans. I don't think that slaves were sold from East Africa, but some people want to blame us. We really do need somebody that can understand how we women suffer."

Her voice took an urgent tone, "I couldn't think of another way, but she needs help. My sister said that maybe God sent you here to help women; some are desperate."

I wanted to get back to Anne's situation—it was difficult to grasp. There was a certain kind of heaviness that appeared to have come over Naomi, and I did not fully understand it.

I said, "Did you notice that coughing studded the air from the mother and someone inside the house? The 12-year-old boy was the only one who did not cough."

"Yes! That's just what I'm saying, it's such a shame somebody can do a person like this... even if his wife did wrong, but I can't see what wrong the girl did." She further commented, as an afterthought, "All that's left for this young girl is to die."

Obviously, Naomi felt passionate about the abuse the young mother received. As for Naomi, she was a married mother of three sons, owned a brick structured compound. Her husband worked with the power and light company, and she worked at a university.

Naomi explained, "You can't understand how it is here. This girl has been rejected, sent back to her mother... like fruit somebody selects but then throws it back like it is rotten. This has brought dishonor to her family."

Naomi also stated, "With me? I could never go back to my mother no matter how badly I was treated; sometimes women just have to endure, by faith."

I commented, "In our marriages, many women would go straight back to their mother, if a marriage has serious problems, whether the husband likes it or not."

There was a brief silence, before she gave a sobering response, which enabled me to realize Anne's circumstances were crucial.

Naomi began, "In Kenya, that kind of thing is not possible. As a child, just a small girl, most African women look forward to getting married, get ourselves a husband and children; full stop. There's nothing more to look forward to in Kenya, and once the dowry is paid, the girl belongs to her husband's family. His mum is hers; his dad, her dad, like that. In some tribes, if the wife tries to leave, the family might stone her.

"See, your culture is different. You don't understand that some of us would rather die than go through such humiliation, as this girl is doing. Have you read in our newspapers, how girls douse themselves with paraffin and strike a match?" She said.

Afterwards, we walked on in our own thoughts, and agreed upon a day to meet again, as our paths divided and she went her way. However, the letter was not written until the next day, Sunday afternoon, and mailed to Daily Nation Letters to the Editor. The Lord led me to make an appeal to 'caring Kenyans' to help the young mother, but I also warned women to beware of the carrier of TB.

Monday, I hand-delivered the same letter to PARENTS magazine. The editor was out but I left the letter for her attention. Desperation propelled me. I had to get the story about Anne publicized; unfortunately, I did not foresee that the dual submission could set off a controversy with the press.

Early Tuesday, Njoroge telephoned me. "This place is going crazy," he said, "Your letter tops the Editorial Page heading: WOMEN MUST BE WARNED OF THIS MAN, but you didn't give us a contact. Two hours after the Daily Nation was on the streets, this place was flooded with calls about the letter. My boss had to assign one person to answer just those calls about the woman with TB."

When I told him to give Charles' box number and thanked him for calling, he had more astonishing news to brighten my morning. **Indeed, our God has never been known to turn His back.**

"I'm afraid you'd betta come down here to Nation House," Njoroge stated, "because a business-man from India dropped off a check for 10,000/shillings and the meat company has given a gift certificate good for one year of sausage, Blue Band margarine and cooking fat. Then an anonymous person gave 7000/cash."

Eve Atenio overheard the conversation and was eager to share her morning paper, and to discuss the story.

She said, "I didn't know that you worked in Umoja, too. You'll find lots of women in the same predicament: men humiliate the girl once the cultivation is finished."

"I am saddened by the case, but I must hurry because Daily Nation is holding money donated to Anne—I thank God for this overwhelming response in her behalf."

Just as I started out the door, another phone call came for me from the editor of the PARENTS magazine. She did not sound pleased.

"Hallo! This is Mary at <u>PARENTS</u> magazine. Are you the one that left a letter for me about the lady in Umoja then you gave the same story to the <u>Daily Nation</u>?"

"Y-yes, I am the one." I admitted, "I meant no harm, it's just that the letter was mailed to them, but I delivered the one for you, without knowing if <u>Daily Nation</u> would use it. All I wanted was to get help as soon as possible."

"Wel-ll, I'm not going to get into any competition with the <u>Nation</u>, we don't do business like that. I called to say that we would accept the story, but then I saw it in the morning newspaper," the editor said.

"Truly, I am sorry. Again, I apologize to you. If I get another story, may I submit it, in case you might be interested?"

"Yes," she replied, "I don't promise to use it. But I'm willing to see what you have; leave it at my office, I'll get back to you, if I want it."

Hurriedly, I contacted Gloria to accompany me to her husband's office and to tell the good news to Anne. About noon, we reached Umoja and found only the mother.

Gloria inquired as to whether Anne had given birth. The mother said that she did not think so, but could not be sure. A tired countenance and deepened eyes from famine told secrets concealed in the 44-year-old grandmother's heart. With both hands rubbing her lower back, she reported on the situation with Anne.

"This morning" (she said in Kikuyu), "three nuns who saw the newspaper came to get Anne, and they took her to Kenyatta Hospital, to keep her from being so far away when it's time to have the baby."

Also, she said that a <u>Kenya Times</u> journalist had been there and told her something about the <u>Daily Nation</u> sitting on a story, and not telling President Moi about it so that he could help them. Gloria and I left to go and find Anne, but I felt a bit uneasy.

"What did the mother say about the <u>Nation</u> had held this story?" I asked, "How could such misunderstanding come about?"

"Please, Mum," Gloria said, "try not to get upset with what these people do here in Kenya. *This man* in State House likes such stories to be told to him; when the public hears it on the Tele, it's praising what the president does to help indigent families."

She added, "He gets annoyed at the editor of <u>Daily Nation</u> then bans it for weeks, if their version of a story doesn't make him look good. Moi favors the <u>Kenya Times</u>."

"I don't want to make trouble. But now, as for <u>PARENTS</u>, I can understand the editor's point, but you can help me to get something else for her. Remember, you once mentioned a girl you know whose cousin is disabled. Can she introduce me to the cousin? It may be a story that Mary might decide to use."

"In fact," Gloria said, "we can do that this week."

At the hospital, in an isolated area, Anne seemed amazed at all that was happening in her behalf. The Catholic nuns had left instructions for all cost incurred by the young mother to be billed to them. Anne said that she never knew that strangers could care so much about her.

She asked us to take part of the money to buy clothes and blanket for the baby, also a robe and house slippers for herself, but to keep the rest of the money until she left the hospital. She said that the baby was overdue; labor would not be induced because she didn't a have a razor blade.

Puzzled, I asked, "What does 'razor' mean in Swahili or is it Kikuyu?"

Gloria smiled and answered, "Its 'RA-ZOR blade" like in English."

"She doesn't need a razor blade," I said, "explain to her there are scissors and scalpels in the Delivery Room when a baby is born in a hospital."

"Mum," Gloria laughed and said, "It is YOU who can't understand. Kenya Government runs this hospital; all pregnant women have to bring their own razor. She is lucky to have a cot; most women just get a thin foam mattress on the floor. Those who may have insurance are placed two in a bunk size bed; one at the head, other at the foot."

We went outside the hospital where several kiosks were set up, bought one razor blade and took it to Nancy. Afterwards, we left the hospital to follow Anne's instructions to buy clothes for the baby.

Eventually, the government offered free education to Anne's five- and six-year olds; the local chief in Umoja ordered the father to pay child support; follow-up treatment cured Anne, and "Baby Maggie" was born free of tuberculosis.

Soon after, the editor of <u>PARENTS</u> accepted the next story that I submitted. My letter gave a brief description of 'Pauline's affliction:

IS THERE HOPE FOR PAULINE? *Now that doctors have given up on treating her, church people stopped coming to pray, sympathizers' visits are few, and the money is all finished, is 27-year-old Pauline's hope for better health in vain?*

The tragic story began in 1984, when her joints started to swell. Throughout 1985-86, doctors at Kenyatta Hospital evaluated her condition; she was operated on and a piece of metal inserted into her hip joint. Three months later, Pauline was completely paralyzed and has been bed-ridden ever since.

She and her family took courage and did not give up. In 1987, a chiropractor diagnosed the disease to be a 'nerve problem and could be treated with therapy.' After paying thousands of shillings, Pauline's condition continued to deteriorate, her morale declined. Out of desperation, the family turned to various herbal doctors, and witch-doctors, but received no meaningful results.

The <u>PARENTS</u> Editor investigated details of my letter and featured Pauline's story in a five-page spread. As a result, churches held fund-raisers, clergymen came to encourage the family and well-wishers donated money. Several doctors offered free therapy—through which, God provided more movement in Pauline's limbs.

So great were the contributions, along with a wheelchair, that the family was able to build a home, and provided private quarters for Pauline. It was a season that God moved mightily in behalf of two desperately helpless young women.

The blessing season continued. With tithes from Gloria, two sisters in our fellowship and mine, we bought food for the poor outside Kibera. On Christmas Eve '91, we delivered food and clothes boxes to five families and four more families on Christmas morning. In one house, there appeared to be about two tablespoons of greens boiling in a half pot of water, meant to feed mother and six children—all under age six.

Still, at another place a baby was sopping some kind of broth with ughali (much like unsalted hot water cornbread). We rejoiced because our boxes contained: potatoes, tomatoes, onion, cabbages, carrots, rice, flour, cooking oil and a chunk of beef. In addition, we left 100 shillings, at each place, in order to buy coal to cook the food.

As God would have it, Mama Monica's husband Peter received Christ in his life and it brought a dramatic change to their home. Peter sent his wife to me to inquire about an issue of marriage. The two had a traditional marriage: dowry was paid and the couple began to live together. Up to then, this arrangement had been sufficient for them.

Mama Monica explained, "Since Peter has gotton Jesus, he wants you to help us marry the *Bible way*—a church, with marriage papers where we may sign our names. In my heart, I also feel that we should do it right, while we have you in Kenya; you know how these things should be done."

"I'll be delighted to arrange it for you," I said, "the passed nine years have been marked by 'for worse' and maybe you can now experience the 'for-better' in marriage."

I was as excited as if it had been one of my daughters. Pastor Mwenba agreed to do the ceremony, and with Gloria's assistance, we planned the whole event, including the wedding dinner. First I bought a used suit for Peter. Only on the wedding day, I learned that a necktie was something he had seen, but had never worn in his 35 years.

A two-piece lace dress that I had was a good fit for the bride, with the skirt band rolled up to shorten it. Strokes of a hot comb on her soft, medium-length brown hair enhanced her heart shaped face. We topped off the effort with a flower bouquet for the lovely bride. She was a natural beauty; disfigured only by poverty.

A minister in our fellowship agreed to act as best man for Peter, and Gloria stood with Mama Monica. After the ceremony and the Marriage Certificate signed, Njoroge drove the wedding party back to his home where the dinner was prepared. No one noticed that

I was the groom's mother and the mother of the bride, at the same time.

In turn, Mama Monica arranged with other mothers to give me some needed assistance. The women wanted to buy fruits and vegetables for me; it cost much more when I purchased them.

One mother said. "The price of onions, tomatoes and fruit will double any time a hawker recognize your accent. What costs me two or three shillings, will be six for you."

In the beginning, what first appeared to have been a simple act had turned into a valuable lesson. It seemed only right to reimburse the mothers when they purchased fruit and vegetables for me with their own money; I saw it as a fair exchange.

I shared this with a young lady in our fellowship, but she saw it with a totally different view. In fact, her comments were unsettling.

"Ohoo, how selfish of you," the young woman said, "you are depriving these women from the blessing that comes with giving to others."

I tried to defend my attitude, "No, these women don't have any money to spend on me, and it wouldn't be right for me to let them buy, and not pay them back. But two of them always refuse to take the money—it's a real problem."

"Sustah Maggie, that is very selfish because you want all the blessings for giving to them; you will not let them get blessed. This is all that they could possibly offer you."

Therefore, I came to realize that I had come to Kenya to teach, as well as to be taught. Indeed, there is a time to give and a time to take; there were lessons to be learned on all sides. From then on, the Kibera mothers continued to assist me in getting produce.

6. WHILE DESTINY PREVAILED

One evening, Eve keenly eyed me as I sewed a Latch Hook craft design. She had many questions because she viewed me as someone who usually has two or three projects going on at the same time.

"What's this you're doing now?" Eve said, "It's very beautiful—but you couldn't have found such a thing here in Kenya, did you?"

"Actually, it was my hobby in the U.S., and it gives me something to do when I get home from school. It's so easy and relaxing because it requires a simple hook, yawn wool and it comes with a pattern."

During the periods that school was out, I asked God to show me how to help mothers to get food for their family. An unusual means was provided through the latch hook handcraft kits. Since no major equipment was needed to sew the craft, it would be an easy process to train the women.

When it seemed my landlady was so much interested in the sewing, and if she had not seen such a craft, others may not have seen it either. I thought a market could be found for the colorful wall hangings and area rugs, so I registered and implemented the handcraft project, as Kibera One Accord Crafts.

This helped me to create jobs and train illiterate and poor mothers to sew the craft; we would sell them house-to-house, and mothers were paid for each craft they had completed. Once the mothers understood how to work the hook, three or four came to my house twice a week. They were glad to earn money for their family and had begun to have a sense of accomplishment and excitement over learning something new.

The Minister for Technical Training, who helped me before, promised us an opportunity to display our crafts at the Nairobi International Show. He was proud of our craft and thought that it would impress the president.

Some times as we worked, the mothers told of horrible experiences with birth control, with pills that disagreed with their body system, month-long hemorrhages and unbearable pain from improperly placed diaphragms. Husbands would say 'it's better to have a baby.'

The mother's growing confidence permitted me to inquire about traditional practices; unlike any other chance I could find. They appeared to be eager to discuss African customs with me. With varied ethnic backgrounds and intermarriages, a wife may be of one tribe, the husband of another; each would bring different tribal practices into the marriage.

If one was from a tribe that circumcised their young girls, and if it happened to be the husband's side, there was little the wife could say against it. Such a custom supported the belief that to cut away the clitoris prevented a woman from becoming a prostitute, and made her faithful to fill her purpose in serving her husband's comfort and pleasure. A Woman's sexual gratification was not worthy of consideration.

Two of the mothers revealed that they had no problem with circumcising girls because they said that 'a girl can get herself a husband faster, if she is circumcised.'

Others firmly promised to not let their daughters *'go under the knife,'* if possible to prevent it. Those who professed Christianity felt it was a sin to force pre-teens girls to be *cut;* although, the practice was deeply embedded in tribal traditions in Africa.

Kenya women were not in the habit of grumbling; since provisions were meager, survival demands occupied their time and effort. With remarkable stamina, women did most of the work in and outside of the house, and would dig with bare hands to plant, weed and harvest crops to sell.

Unfortunately, Kenyan fathers give land only to sons; it was a rare thing for a daughter to inherit land from her parents. Women could work the land but not own it. Theirs was a daily grind. Money from welfare, food stamps or payments for child-support did not exist.

Therefore, anything they could do with their hands meant another meal, for one more day. No cabinets were necessary in a one-room Kibera home; a stark reality was that they had no extra dishes—or food—to store up. Probably, no more than fifty out of a thousand families could afford to eat a full meal, on a regular basis.

"Although there are tribal differences," Mama Lucy said, "most tribes believe that once a woman gets married, it's expected that she gets pregnant in the first year. The longer it takes her to get a baby, the more suspicion arises that she is barren, and therefore, cursed."

Mama Mark added, "Like my husband's tribe believes: If a wife does not get pregnant within two years, she is considered useless and may be replaced."

"Replaced, how?" I asked.

"Like, my mother-in-law could bring her son another wife, if I could not give him children. I know of girls who were stoned and driven away while the husband was at work and a replacement was brought. So the new girl would prepare a fine meal, make herself look beautiful then wait for the man to come back home."

Mama Mark continued, "His mother tells him, 'that useless wife of yours has run away, but the one I have brought you is healthy and can give you children.' That's it!"

Once I asked the mothers, "If God granted you one wish, what would you ask?"

Their responses varied: To have plenty food and education for their children, and a job was unanimous among the group. Mama Monica had a strange request to God.

The 32-year-old in a threadbare blouse and frayed kanga, simply asked for one thing. "I wish God to help me to get a *curtain*."

I said, "Your one wish to God is to get a CURTAIN?"

Mama Monica tried to explain. "My husband works outside Nairobi and can come home just one weekend out of a month. The three children, the oldest is eight, do not always fall asleep early enough in our one-room place, when the father is at home."

She said that it was difficult to convince her husband to wait for the children to sleep; it was not a priority to him. She added, "Some husbands are impatience, but to hang a curtain between us and the children would make it not so bad."

I stated, "Your request is so humble, may God bless you to get a bigger house."

Although some of the women felt that they were not important enough for God to listen to their prayers, I tried to explain their value to Him.

"The only reason I am in your country is because the heavenly Father loves you so much—He is a Father Who cares."

One of the mothers looked stunned and said, "How can you say such a thing? We Africans have suffered famine, ethnic wars, Colonial Rule for many generations. You are talking to us about a 'loving Father,' but we're told most about hell fire and punishment."

"Ladies, I don't claim to have answers to all your questions. Greedy and evil politicians bring about some things, but I'm quite sure God love Kenyans. He sent me to give you that message, across lands and oceans to assure you of HIS love."

Mama Daniel was troubled by something I did, which she felt was a big sin; through an interpreter she inquired about the earrings in my ears.

"Sustah Maggie, she is asking 'why do you wear earrings and it was taught to us, from missionaries long ago, that only prostitutes wear such jewelry—to tempt men.'"

"I will certainly answer her question, if she will answer a question for me, first?

Does she believe that it was God that sent me to Kenya to help the people of Kibera?"

When Mama Daniel was given the questions, she vigorously nodded her head and smiled, with her eyes up to the ceiling, as to signal her thanks to God. Then I gave a response to her question to me.

"On the day I was praying and God said that I had to come to Nairobi, I was wearing earrings on my ears. He never said that I should remove them before I arrived here. But I definitely believe that <u>anything</u> can be taken too far. I doubt if you'll hear any message preached on 'TEMPERANCE' because we must use restraint in most areas of behavior. It could be in the way we dress, makeup, talk, eat, drink, and so forth."

Mama Monica admitted that she felt unsure and fearful of being in the Annual Nairobi International Show, but was willing to go. She had never seen President Moi in his 17 years in office, because they could not afford electricity, or even buy newspapers.

I said, "No need to worry, if the president stops at our display, I will show you what to do. According to Gloria, if he stops, it's possible that he would allocate land for us to have a better place to expand and work. We'll see when the day comes."

Meanwhile, five young Americans visited Kenya from a Catholic university in Illinois; an AC pastor referred them to me for insight about conditions for women. I agreed to tell them about my work in Kibera. Their African tour included Somali and Tanzania and to see how the women were treated in Third World Countries.

Three of the students that visited me showed interest in getting a fellow- American's perspective. After I served them refreshments, we began to talk in general about deprivations in Kibera Village. A student named Tammy began the discussion.

She asked, "How badly are the women treated in Kenya and what do you plan to do about it?" Tammy had a definite mission, and eagerly anticipated my reply.

"How bad it is would depend on the standard by which it is measured. In Africa, it's not just a 'woman's problem' but a human issue that is steeped in lack of education, insufficient food and failed government strategies in which people can't maintain a decent living. Sure, there are women lawyers, educators and doctors, but more should be allowed to run—and win–political races. My role in Kenya is not political."

Tammy said, "We are in the forefront of demanding changes for women, starting with the Bible. Wherever 'he' in Scripture refers to God, we want it changed so that it does not reflect a gender— replaced by titles like the 'Power, Source or the Force.'"

Tammy talked fast and barely took a breath as she said, "You may be aware of our gain in getting more respect for Mother Earth. I think you could be very effective in mobilizing women in this important historical effort. I can send you litera...."

I interrupted, "As said before, I'm not here to oppose the Kenya Government. I'm here to tell individuals—a woman, a man, a child, day-to-day, about the love of the Father and that HE sent HIS Son that we may know HIS unconditional love. Also, no matter who disagrees or what writings are altered, my prayers will always be addressed to our "Father-God."

Her eyes reflected pity for me. In a patronizing tone, Tammy said, "Wel-ll, many people feel like you do, but we're trying to enlighten them. I think, even you can recognize that such talk does nothing about issues of female circumcision, poliga..."

"My view differs with yours. When I tell a mother that God loves the children so much that it hurts Him to see girls mutilated, not one mother can allow it to happen, without remembering how God feels about it. My message goes directly to the home, the sitting room—at breakfast or tea time. Decades of tribal traditions do not go away overnight."

† † † † †

Without notice, months had rapidly passed, and I went to renew my two-year Work Permit. The Social Services Director told me of a growing problem in the Social Service School for Disabled Children. Help was badly needed in several areas.

The school did a fine job, but some parents believed that a disabled child could not be educated; of course, they struggled with too little help and seriously limited funds. No help was available from the government and when donations and foreign aid were given, other priorities soaked up the money.

Early on, during my travels around Nairobi, I had met the Chairman of Kenya Society of the Disabled. A friendship had developed between us, and it gave me an opportunity to discuss with him the problems at the school.

The Chairman invited me to come on his live television show to talk to parents on the air, and to make an appeal for donors. The school's director and I were guests on Voice of Kenya (VOK) Community News. A few businessmen and organizations contacted the chairman to offer support for the worthy cause of the school.

The day of the Nairobi International Show, Gloria, Mama Monica and I were stationed at our booth. Gloria arranged our crafts in a colorful and decorative display on a table and the wall behind us, in hopes to sell them. The mothers had made framed wall hangings, cushioned pillows and area rugs with skid-proof backing.

Even if President Moi should observe the display tables next to us, it was no guarantee he would stop at ours; he might still skip over to another isle. The nervous mother was cautioned not to get too excited, and to remember to do as we had planned.

Jua Kali (one who works in the sun) entrepreneurs stood at their displays which included wood-carving; African Art and Artifacts and various styles of handbags. Our craft was one of a kind, in four different designs. Participants were allowed to sell or take orders from visitors in the pavilion, once the president had left the show.

The face of every craftsman showed intense hope and anticipation and our hearts were saying *'please, Your Excellency, stop by my stall.'* The presidential entourage consisted of his personal bodyguard, Kenya's most popular TV anchorwoman, cameraman, high-ranking government ministers, military officers and reporters from foreign and domestic newspapers.

As they came closer—just four stalls away from us, the hairs were standing up on back of my neck and on my arms. I nudged Mama Monica to alert her to get ready; she took the latch hook in her hand. The three of us stood rigidly straight—barely breathing.

In moments, the entourage was standing at our display and looking down at the various crafts. With scepter in his right hand, President Daniel arap Moi stood directly in front of Mama Monica; the anchorwoman, the military brass and cameraman inched in for a closer look.

"Your Excellency," she began (in Kiswahili), "this is a craft I have learned how to do with my hands. May I show you how it is done?"

President Moi slightly nodded to signal her to proceed. She did exactly as had been shown to her, and smiled during the process. Everything was hushed. All eyes focused on the president and Mama Monica; for just about sixty seconds, she was one of the most important women in Kenya—she held the president's attention.

She continued, "Your Excellency, we are in Kibera, but we don't have space to make enough crafts to compete in the market."

He replied, "I will come to look in on you. What name are you under?"

"Kibera One Accord Crafts, Your Excellency," she answered with eyes downcast and her head lowered.

In less than three minutes, she had seen and had face-to-face dialogue with the president of her country. The entourage moved on; ecstatic clapping and dancing erupted at our table, Mama Monica was awe-struck. That day, most of our craft were sold before we left the Pavilion, and several merchants wanted to make wholesale orders.

Mama Monica tried to express her feelings, "Mum-mee, I see you... like a personal angel God gave to my family... I don't know all who else you helping... but God sent you to us—*for sure.*" Tears streaming down her face, she said, "My children, who could not pass school gates, now they have sponsor and a seat in the class... somebody like ME can talk to the president... God had you to bring us this chance."

"I told you before, it is God's work because He loves you, I didn't know you and had never heard the word 'Kibera' so give God all the thanks. He'll be here for you, long after I've returned to the United States."

In 1992, we won first place for best craft display at the Annual Jual Kali Show in Mombasa. President Moi presented to us a trophy and Best Craft Certificate. Thereafter, we heard nothing more from him in regard to our crafts.

From time-to-time, it became evident that no training I had previously received in church had adequately prepared me for in-depth mission service. It was not hard to see that service in a foreign country presented issues and challenges that could not be anticipated, unless one has actually lived, a considerable time, outside amenities provided in developed countries.

A friend in England sent me a box of used children's clothing, all in excellent condition. The postal clerk charged 1600/shillings for duty charges, in order for me to collect the package. I had no such amount and hot tears burned my eyes. I stood at the Customs counter and tried to think of a solution; images of Kibera children came into my mind, I refused defeat. When I explained my work to a supervisor, it fell on deaf ears.

I gave a verbal lashing to the Customs Officer, "Why do you people make it so hard for your poor to be helped? You won't help them yourselves and you harass others who come to Kenya to try to make a difference—SHAME on you!"

"Mad-dam," the officer said, "I have rules that must be followed, and there are taxes and duty fees. You should know that the cost of these things has recently gone up."

When I noticed three young Japanese, an Indian couple, and several Americans gather around to show me support in the issue, I would not be appeased.

"Some things should be an exception," I continued, "I'm trying to help the poor Kibera children and you're charging me more than the cost when the clothes were new,"

Others joined in; by the time we finished with him, I was given the package for 270/. There is still a place and time for *righteous indignation.*

Meanwhile, John Mwenba who was Secretary of the Assemblies of Christ assisted me in renewal of the Work Permit. Not only did he have a well-paid job as a Customs Officer, best of all, he was married to a Kalenjin (the president's tribe). Kalenjins and their spouses were, allegedly, given favor in jobs throughout the country.

Beginning in 1992, Pastor Mwenba and I worked together as co-founders of the Nairobi Gospel Center (NGC), an English-speaking worship service; this eliminated the need for interpretation. We started out in a small meeting room of a local university, as the membership grew, on Sundays we rented the dinning room of a large restaurant.

Approximately, 200 baptized believers regularly attended, and I scheduled quarterly meetings with the young wives and mothers. Soon after we started, it became evident that many of our members were experiencing heart-rending problems, and they longed for solutions from the Lord.

Young brides agonized over not getting pregnant; rampant death toll of AIDS impacted thousands of families and others tried all possible methods to find a job; others needed to be delivered from abusive homes. It was then that an assignment was given to me to carry out from July 1 through 31st.

The Lord said, **"Fast and Pray in behalf of believers whose trials require a sustained prayer assault against the enemy; take request from those who find it difficult to spend enough time in prayer as they desire."**

Half way through July, some graduates from universities in France, London and New Delhi returned home to Kenya and 20 of them joined our fellowship. Kenyans from ages 25-40 appreciated the chance to regularly use English.

It was announced that prayer requests could be given to me, in confidence. Out of the new group, I particularly remember three young adults who gave their requests.

Twenty-six-year old Joyce wrote her request and gave it to me. She had earned her bachelor degree, and felt that God wanted her to start a women's group when she returned to Kenya. First, she would need a job to pay for registration and other costs. Her request was to find employment.

Daniel was about 22, and his prayer request consisted of ten things. His list had begun with a trip to the USA for further studies, a good-paying job, get a Christian wife; tenth on his list was for sinners in his family to accept Christ.

Most memorable was 31-year-old Brenda, who wished to find a place to move away from her parents. She had received a grant to study for a doctorate, but she was the youngest of eight children;

peace and a quiet place could not be found when nieces and nephews came to visit their grandparents.

I asked, "Do you get along well with your parents?"

"Oh, yes," she said, "I have a loving relationship with both my parents. It's only that I can't afford to lose my grant, so I need to be able to concentrate and study."

"I will tell you exactly what the Lords gives to me, whether it is what you want to hear or not. People sometimes want God to say only the things that they like," I said.

Moments after I walked away from Brenda, I heard these words: *Tell her not to move.* Still, I had promised to pray and I would do so. All week long I prayed. For Daniel, I was given one statement: The Holy Spirit is appalled that salvation for loved ones was Daniel's last concern. The messages to Brenda remained: Tell her not to leave; this is not the time. I received nothing else.

Before the month's end, two of our couples testified that they were expecting a child by April, in the coming year; one brother found part-time work, two girls would soon start training for full-time jobs.

The last Sunday in July, Joyce met me at the church door with news of her scheduled interview for a job. At the end of the morning worship, I went to Daniel and explained the reply given for him. One of his habits was to stress that 'Jesus can come any day' but his family's salvation was last on his list of ten desires.

Next, in private I said to Brenda, "I'm not sure if the message for you is good or bad, but the Holy Spirit said, *'you should not move from your parents' home; this is not the time.'*"

With a puzzled look, Brenda asked, "Why not? What is wrong with my desire to have a place of my own? It is the only way, if I am to be successful in my studies."

"Sister Brenda," I replied, "you're an adult and can do what you want to do—I'm just telling you that I feel God has said "no" to your request to move. But its okay, I think, to ask the Lord to let you know when the time is right; He will guide you."

Brenda said that if she had not planned to accept the answer, there would have been no need for her to submit a prayer request.

Thereafter, I had no further conversation with those three young members; the matter was left between them and God.

Two other older brides who wanted to get pregnant testified their good news. In all, eight in our fellowship found employment. Towards the end of September, plans were underway to celebrate our second anniversary, as Nairobi Gospel Center.

Visitors often came by to request that I come to their church as guest speaker; sometimes two or three would come. When six young women from our fellowship came, it was quite unusual. The women chatted and laughed as they came through the gate, walked into the sitting room and found seats for themselves. A minister's wife was the first to speak, as the traditional hand shaking and Kiswahili greetings begin.

"Sustah Maggie, we have come with some good news and some NOT so good. Now, which one do you want us to tell first?"

"Well, I probably prefer to hear the 'not so good' then the good."

"Okay, three people from our fellowship will no longer be worshipping with us."

"Oh! Why is that—have they left the country? Or found another church?"

"Now, that brings the good news." After a pause, with a sober look she added, "They have gone to be with the Lord."

As I struggled to get the realization of her comment, seconds of silence passed. I grasped for the meaning to make sure that I understood; she nodded to my questions. "What are you saying–three of our members have gone? They're d-dead? Do I know them?"

Another sister explained: A group had gone up-country to hold open-air services, on their trip back to Nairobi two matatus collided at a blind curve on Thika Road. One vehicle flipped over the side of the road and six people died instantly. The names of three of them left me seriously shaken.

Joyce lived only two hours, after being taken to the hospital; others died at the scene, Daniel was one. Then the minister's wife continued the story.

"Our dear Sustah Brenda was among those who did not make it; she died."

AN EAR TO HEAR

The shock of the news, and that we had five 'Brendas' in our congregation, caused me difficulty in registering the news in my mind, as to just which woman it was.

"Do I know *this* Brenda?" I asked.

"Yes! You remember in July, she is the one that wanted to move from her parents' house... you told her not to move... it was not the time."

"Bu-but did she move?" I inquired.

In unison, nearly all six women answered, "No! She did not."

Chill bumps swept over my body and I said, "Thank God! He knew that she would never have gotten that degree; it was more important for her to spend time with her loving parents... no wonder, the Spirit said it was not the time."

Unfortunately, not all situations ended with such a positive outlook. Just three years after Anne's story was in the newspapers, I received a shocking report when Naomi came to see me about one of her own personal problems.

On a cold July Sunday evening, Naomi found me home ironing clothes for the coming week, while the electricity was on. The news she brought sounded good on the surface with respect to Anne, but it gave me a *kick* in the stomach *stab* in the heart.

After we greeted each other, Naomi went directly to the point of her visit.

"I am here to tell you that this girl, Anne, is back with the husband."

Instantly, one hand flew over my mouth then I said, "That is horrible, p-please, Naomi, tell me it isn't so. It can't be true!" I felt hot tears and cold disbelief.

She said, "I couldn't believe it either, but we must not think too harshly about her—it's really not her fault. As you know, she cannot read; therefore, when the government sent a letter for the chief to make the husband pay support money, the chief took bribes from Nancy's husband."

"So," she added, "when the chief read the Permanent Secretary's letter to Anne, he lied and said that free education for the children and child support came with a requirement for her to be reconciled with her husband."

"Does she want TB again? Or to get kicked out when he sees the donations are finished? How could the chief do such a thing?" Disgust invaded my spirit.

"Aaah, Sustah Emma, bribe money will get whatever you want here in Kenya. Now she wants the rest of the money that she asked you to keep."

"I had hoped the remaining 5000/shillings could be used to pay school fees for Baby Maggie, but if Anne wants it now, I'll have to give it to her. Tell her to meet me Monday at Barclay's Bank by noon. I am deeply sorry this has happened."

Afterwards, Naomi told me something more personal that saddened her. The husband's youngest brother had had a mental breakdown, just as he planned to sit for final exams to graduate from the University of Nairobi. The pressure from family is so great on university students to successfully complete school, and to get a good job, some commit suicide and others break under the strain.

Naomi said, "The family has spent so much on medicines and doctors, and it has not helped, even though we tried herbalists and even a witch-doctor. My husband and I agreed to ask you to come and pray for him."

"Does he understand that I am coming to pray for him?"

"We have told him that we would find someone who can really help because none of the others did anything to cure him. Now we need God to help us."

The next day my first stop was to meet Anne at the bank. She no longer needed spoon-feeding as a down-trodden wife; in her mind, she was again a blossoming giddy bride. Her interpreter appeared to disagree with what Anne was about to do.

The lady said, "All a man has to do is to pretend to love this silly girl, and she can not listen to nothing else; Madame, you just can't help some people."

The evening I arrived at Naomi's home, the 22-year-old student sat quiet and still on her sofa. When he was introduced to me, he sat motionless with a wide-eyed blank stare, but did not reply. As I began to pray, standing a foot away from him, the Lord told me to lay my hands on the young man's head.

AN EAR TO HEAR

Quietly, I asked Naomi, "Will he mind if I put my hands on his head?"

"I-it's OK, he can understand what you're saying—just carry on."

Immediately, with my hands on his head, I briefly prayed in my *prayer language;* the young man was unresponsive. Before I left the home, I cautioned the family to not take the boy again to a witch-doctor, and to wait for **God to do His work.**

Three weeks later, a friend and I were strolling along in City Centre, when she called my attention to a man waving and walking towards us. He did not look familiar to me, but as he approached us, he said to my friend in Kiswahili that he knew me and that I should recognize him, also. Then he turned to me and started to speak in English.

"Sustah, so you don't remember me now? I am John."

"You know, I meet many people, but it's hard to remember all..."

Abruptly, he said, "But you came to pray for me and yet you can't remember? I didn't know how to find you to say that I got healed; I've already sat for my exams."

"Ooo, you're Naomi's brother-in-law. Praise the Lord!! You are all right now?"

"Yes! I have passed all my exams and the graduation is in two weeks. If I invite you, will you come as my guest to Nairobi University?"

"Yes, of course, I've not attended a university graduation, since I came to Kenya. But I must be there to help you to celebrate a *double* victory. I surely hope that you've told the Lord 'thank You' for how He delivered you."

"In fact," unashamed, he said, "I wanted to laugh out loud when you touch my head and started saying all that funny stuff *in tongues*, but the next morning, I could see that I was healed. I went back to school because if I had waited two more days, it would have been too late to take my exams."

Once again, God had proven Himself so that the weak can say 'I'm strong.' We parted, and I promised to attend, if he got an invitation for me. It was marvelous how God had blessed him. At the graduation, I was proud and even more thankful that I was able to attend because no members of his family were present.

7. WHEN IT MIRRORS UGLINESS

My friend Rachel (I called my angel) seldom visited, but there seemed to have been definite purpose whenever she did come. She wanted me to accompany her to a small private hospital, so that we could pray for a woman said to have a liver disease. Doctors did not expect the young lady to live out the weekend.

It was the first time I had seen such a condition: her fingers and toenails were black and dark patches were on her face and balding spots on the scalp.

Rachel said to the patient, "We have come to visit and to pray, my son tells me that you believe Jesus can heal you. This is my friend from America, and she is also a servant of the Lord."

We prayed and gave encouraging words to the 27-year-old patient, and as we left, Rachel said that we had one more stop to make. After two bus rides, we arrived at a place that looked to be an old warehouse. Sisters from a Kenya Convent had rented it to use as part of their prison ministry. Sister Maria escorted us and told about their work and how they were trying to make a difference.

She said, "We saw that it was not enough to minister to the women behind prison walls, but something was badly needed to assist them when they re-entered society. We started out with 50 rebuilt sewing machines and rolls of material at wholesale prices, and set up this workshop."

Rachel asked, "Is it for all the women, if they want to participate."

"Oh no, Sister Hannah, our director, allows only women who attended Mass, accepted counseling and showed sincere interest in a new life while yet in prison. So when they are paroled, we meet them as they walk out prison doors, and train them in tailoring—not just the basics, but several have become fine tailors."

"How do they manage once they leave your program? In what way do they gain complete independence?" I ask.

"Once they reach intermediate training stage, a girl can begin to buy a sewing machine from us by installments and when she completes the program, we give them two rolls of material. This way, the student can sell the garments she makes here then use the material to make other garments to get off to a good start."

"Sister Maria," I said, "some may have no place to stay while they attend the class so does this shut them out of the program?"

"Upstairs, there are six bunk beds—two girls to a bed, and a kitchen, but if a woman does not move through the steps of training in three months, she is discharged from our program. Sister Hannah designed the training so that they MUST show progress because we're not equipped for permanent residency."

As Rachel and I left to take separates buses to get home, that's when my own unexpected battle began. Discontent overshadowed me in a strong feeling that **I was not doing enough for God**.

I thought: *God! Why, oh why can I not do something like the nuns are doing to help women? If I just had a couple of sewing machines, I could teach the Kibera mothers how to sew many things—this is something I wish to do, but don't have the funds. It is marvelous work the nuns are doing, but I've not made a real difference.*

Although it occurred to me that I was just ONE, and the nuns were many with sufficient resources; that did not help me. The attack continued, as I walked into my house and pouted, *"I'm doing NOTHING compared to the nuns' accomplishments—I feel so inadequate and I'm letting the Kibera women down."*

The Holy Spirit then spoke to me, **"Why are you sad, when God has used you to make other's heart glad? You're where God wants** *you to be, doing what He told you to do, if you're not content then it's not God's name you want praised, but yours."*

My reproof was in the Word of God. II Corinthians 13:11:

"When I was a child, I spoke as a child, I understood as a child, I thought as a child: but when I became mature, I put away childish things."
(KJV).

Blinded by SELF-PROMOTION, pouting and complaining, the Lord had to open my eyes that I might see the hideous ugly spirit of zealous *discontent,* which had come to make sure I was defeated in Kenya. Whenever we want the glory, instead of giving God all the praise, no matter what *size* the task, defeat is inevitable.

Immediately, I asked the Lord for forgiveness. His Word mirrored a self-seeking spirit that retards maturity in Christ. I felt so ashamed. In God's leniency, that ugliness was exposed so that I may be delivered. Kibera was not about ME, the mission was entirely about God's great love for the suffering women and children. It was God's work, God's country; His people.

While reading Luke, Chapter seven (KJV) I began to realize: We are not the Owners; we are the debtors.

All money sent to me belongs to GOD to be used for His purpose. What He put into my hands was not meant for sewing machines, but meant for needy families. There were times He provided money for my needs; another time, it was to pass through my hands to others, even so with the nuns. All of it belonged to God.

Just a few days later, Rachel visited me with amazing news that left me groping to find words of expression to the Lord. Thanks seemed so inadequate.

She said, "Our girl has returned home..."

I interrupted, "But doesn't your daughter live with you already?"

"NO! No, my Sustah, I'm talking about the one we saw at the hospital. Remember? We prayed healing prayers for her."

"Seriously, Rachel, what happened?"

"My God—He is the one Who did it. It is finished! She was released from the hospital today but one (yesterday), and I have come with her message of 'thanks to you.' She will return to work on Wednesday. Oh, my God is mightier than any disease –greater than any other power," she said.

I was still rejoicing, as I read a letter from my daughter Yvonne. In it she wrote a message to me from the Lord: *This mission in Kenya is in a stage similar to photo negatives, everything God does through you now is another picture taken, and all will be developed long after you've returned home.*

"Great is the Lord, and greatly to be praised; and His greatness is unsearchable."
Psalms 145:3 (KJV)

How much more would our Father do through us, if only He could trust us to not take the praise, when God deserves all the glory.

8. ANGELS ACCOMPLISHED THEIR PURPOSE

In my experience, God would speak to me in various ways: through Scripture, words spoken to my heart through the Spirit of Truth, a screen on which I would get instructions, or simply a strong inclination or compelling urge.

Such inclination was felt when I went to the American Embassy to volunteer. Again, I had to make the first step then learn the purpose, in due time.

Smith Hempstone, the American Ambassador to Kenya (at the time) had initiated the Ambassador's Self-Help Fund, within the main embassy. The Self-Help acted as mediator between USAID and the many organizations that requested funds. While my personal work focused more on individual or family help, the Self-Help office gave me a small way to help make sure U.S. dollars reach those who needed it most.

Particularly, the Self-help Office investigated request for funding, and determined if legitimate need existed then made a recommendation to USAID. Less or more money in some cases could be sanctioned for funding, as deemed necessary by the coordinator.

Since a few groups would try to get funding from more than one embassy, for same project, a cross-check list was developed.

Therefore, attempts to get dual funding would be rejected by all embassies contacted.

I worked two to three days a week (depended on the agenda), four to five to hours a day. It was a lot of work to be done, and until I came, Coordinator Beth Norris worked alone. On my third day, I saw it was plenty work to keep both of us busy.

Beth said, "It is hard to believe that someone with office skills could just walk through the door and volunteer." She added, "Discussions have already started as to how to find money to hire you full time."

Because I needed the freedom to continue my personal work I told Beth that I wasn't interested in employment. It was not clear why I was there, yet; on the surface, it was to assist her in office work, but there was more to come.

In our long rides together to the bush areas, Beth and I grew more familiar and we had mutual respect for each other's task. I shared stories about the many marvelous things God did in behalf of the people in Kibera; seldom did a day pass that I shared an eventful story without ended it by saying: "That's just like God."

When Beth participated in groundbreaking ceremonies, I accompanied her, and she showed no annoyance when I told things God was doing to help families. One day as I ended a story with "... just like God," Beth revealed a side I had not noticed.

"To tell you the truth," she said, "I'm not *too sure* about **GOD**. My husband's mother died of cancer, his youngest sister lost a long batter with lung cancer, and recently his only sister was diagnosed with breast cancer."

Beth added, "How can there be a loving God who could allow such anguish and heartbreak? A similar situation exists in my own family—just not as bad."

Her point was clear and I had no answer to ease her doubt. The only response I could give was the discovery in my life, across the years. My assignment to Kenya validated, to me, the existence of a loving Father of the universe.

I said, "All I can say is that things which have taken place in my life were neither accidents, twists of fate, nor coincidences. Kibera is one example, since I had never heard that name before I came to

Kenya, now it seems to have been a major part of my life's purpose. Only an all-wise, omniscient God could have orchestrated it."

In the weeks that followed, I imagined that there were times when God chuckled about Beth and me; an agnostic with a Christian, working together for a common cause. Both of us had equal access to God's love and grace. What an awesome God!

Two weeks before Christmas '93, the bank lost two money orders I had deposited, along with checks meant for schools fees. My account was debited almost 14,200/shillings. Debate with the bank manager, in regard to lost school fees, was of no effect. I contacted my sister Janet for help to get those money orders re-written.

I scrambled feverishly to find money to pay school fees and not lose the students' seat in the classroom. Once lost, a child's seat could not be retrieved because there were so many children and too few schools. As I shared my frustration, Beth offered to help.

She asked, "If you don't mind, just sign the money orders to me and I'll take it to the embassy cashier then bring the cash back to you; sometimes it's up to five shillings more than what banks offer per dollar."

By February, American Express had replaced the lost money orders, and at the time I took them to the Barclay's Bank, the currency exchanged had nearly doubled. The bank had to credit my account over 28,000/shillings for 14,200/ they had debited earlier.

This time, the story created much excitement in the Self-Help office. When Beth heard the whole story of my good fortune, it drew a spontaneous statement from her.

Beth said, "Isn't that just like G... wel-ll... I mean–its funny how such things can happen."

† † † † †

As it happened, my niece had written to me about her move to a newly found fellowship where she worshipped. God had drawn her to the Light of the World Christian Church (LWCC), and she marveled at the difference it was making in her spiritual growth and insight.

The more recent letter from her urged me to tell her pastor about Kibera and see if he may assist. I did follow-up on her suggestion, although I was reluctant, it was a time when the currency exchange was at its highest rate.

About the same time, the government issued a statement that anybody who gave a contribution to youth of the KANU Political Party could be allocated land; if we had the money, the District Officer would designate land, no questions asked.

With only three days left before the cut-off date for land allocation, the LWCC trusted God and sent the largest single contribution, since I had come to Kenya. This made it possible to get enough land to help a widow with two small sons, other families, including Mama Monica's family of five. Earlier, she felt that all she dared to hope for was a *curtain*.

On the allocated land, we bought sand, wood, and other materials for building the family structures, and pay for needed labor. Nearly six years before, those families were not able to regularly pay for use of a latrine; now they owned their two-room house and a private latrine, and their children had education sponsorship.

To go shopping for groceries with money left over, I also arranged a time to meet the mothers in town at Uchumi supermarket. As we neared the store, I noticed how chatty the mothers had become.

One of the women said, "Mumee, we are trying to figure what this big building is used for? I have always wondered what people do inside there."

Mama Monica and the other mothers, all in mid- to late-thirties, had never shopped in a grocery store. They surmised that the supermarket was a government building or Parliament. Since I was from the United States, the women believed that a mother, like me, could better understand why they needed to shop in such places.

November '94, the Lord told me to prepare to go home and pay the fare from my end. As the currency skyrocketed, so did the cost of living; I could not foresee how to save the airfare home with my present income.

By now, I had learned that **a guarded gait is required, if we travel a narrow path.** So I practiced doing what I could, and left the supernatural to God.

More frequently, stories had begun to appear in newspapers about mistreatment of Peace Corps workers, and incidents of beatings and robberies to other foreigners. Kenya politicians' blatant criticism of the American government was not uncommon.

One morning as I arrived at the embassy, Beth said, "My boss suggested that you take more precaution in traveling around the city, and as soon as possible, wrap up your work in the country. Americans' safety in Kenya is waning."

Embassy personnel were confident that the embassy was one of the safest places in Kenya, but considered that their living quarters left them vulnerable. *(Note: None of us knew or could have imagined that in a few years, the American Embassy would be leveled to the ground by a suicide bomber. Because Mrs. Norris had already returned to the United States, I hoped she finally said **'that's just like God.'**)*

Until Beth received a transfer (at her request), to an assignment in the United States, my scheduled continued at the embassy. The last day in the Self-Help Office, Beth mentioned that Italy's Alitalia Airlines gave discount fares to clergymen, and may possibly offer the same to evangelists and mission workers.

After I checked with airlines, I discovered that in less than six more months, I could accumulate enough for a ticket home. One method, I thought, was to save airfare by not cashing the money orders, except for the children's school fees and to curtail travel by remaining close to Nairobi.

The last time Beth cashed money orders I put the ten thousand shillings into a black patent-leather clutch purse, and placed it on the top shelf of my closet. Sixty days later, I put a money order in a drawer, and felt encouraged that airfare was possible, before the end of the year.

Work with the women in our fellowship continued on a regular basis. A young mother from our fellowship came to visit me to discuss a problem that weighed on her heart. She was fearful that she may lose her husband.

"Sustah Maggie," she began, "Minister Obeara's wife told me to talk to you about a serious matter, before you leave Kenya."

The twenty-seven-year-old wife was first hesitant to be specific, until I told her the only way I could help was to hear exactly what was troubling her. It had stemmed from her childhood and now was affecting her adult life.

"Since I was young, my grand mother and the old mamas said that in the Bible the great sin of Adam and Eve was to have sexual intercourse. It makes me feel sinful when my hus-bund wants to have sex."

I said, "But you have two children already so, dear, when did this feeling start?"

"From the very first night, but eets what a wife has to do, and eet has gotton worse, as the years have gone by. In fact, I fear so much that if I die, my soul will go straight to hell fire."

The multiplicity of the problem began when the 31-year-old husband kept away from home, at every opportunity, and had become annoyed by his wife's coldness. The times he was not at work, at least, he was doing things and going places with our pastor.

First I prayed with her, pointed out specific scriptures about Adam and Eve, and let her read it for herself. We read Genesis 1:28 (KJV), and I explained that God's instructions **"Be fruitful and multiply..."** came in Chapter one; the sin came in the third chapter.'"

"As a mother," I added, "I understand that parents tell children—especially girls, things that they feel are *precautions*. The mamas tried to make you fearful enough to not mess up your life before marriage, but they neglected to straighten it out as you grew up."

With astonishment, she read the scripture repeatedly. In amazement, she said, "I can't think that my mother or even my grandmother would know what the Bible *actually* says. Sometimes things are 'just said,' and nobody knows exactly how it got started."

I suggested that when her husband reaches out to her, she should simply remember God's instructions, and enjoy something that's sacred between husband and wife—their bed is not defiled—sex between husband and wife is not sinful.

"Your husband will thank God," I laughed and added, "and in time he might even become glad that you and I had this talk."

A few days later, Naomi and her husband came to visit me and to share a burden on their hearts. In their earlier effort to get help for John, one of the doctors must have use a contaminated needle and John was now HIV positive.

It was not their feeling that John was sexually active, and I believed them because it is not uncommon for young Kenyan men and women to be virgins—-even up to age 30. We talk awhile, prayed together, and then I also asked them a favor.

"God is going to heal John, but he and I need to have a talk, so send him to see me this week. Don't tell him that I know about the HIV—we'll keep in touch."

Two days later, John came for dinner and he did not mention his diagnosis, until he was ready to leave. I felt the need to make my purpose clear for having him to come.

"John, have you given any thought to surrendering your life to God?

"Oh no, I don't have time for that stuff now; I want to have some fun in life, first, later I probably will consider getting in church."

"Just to join a church is not what I mean. Seems like you view God Almighty as just a favor-doer—one to contact when you need a favor. Wel-ll, I'm not the person to help you do that. God blesses because He loves us, but He also wants us to love Him."

A month thereafter, Gloria brought me word that John had been given letters from three doctors at different hospitals to verify that he was no longer HIV positive, but John still showed no concern for his spiritual condition.

Preparation had to be made for my departure. When I first obtained my Work Permit, the Social Service Director asked that I train a Kenyan to serve in same capacity in which I had worked. It was a difficult promise to keep because I was a volunteer; no Kenya could afford to give free service, regardless of the training, or purpose.

Pastor Charles decided to take over as Headmaster, but he found the teachers not willing to take a lesser salary than what I had paid to them. The teachers were aware that more money was coming in and wanted what was due to them. The school had become known as the school that holds graduations; another classroom would soon be completed.

The Kenya experience showed me how critical it is to have an ear to hear the voice of the Lord, and to be willing to obey.

As part of the refining process, rebuke, reproof and instruction will bring about replenished joy and restored strength. Not all that I heard was joyful; some things were hard to bare. There were also times when a word of encouragement was meant to reinforce the faith of others.

Experiences shared in this story may help you to combat your doubts, and reach out to try God, and find that the unfamiliar and timid ones, those behind the scenes, do receive the same favor as the popular and powerful. **Because His love is impartial and unconditional, there are no unimportant people in God's sight**.

At times, when the laity might feel anesthetized by being over-churched and sermon saturated, it is not uncommon for God's people to experience 'burn-out', and to fear whether they are living in His perfect will.

The Lord is faithful to confirm His will in ways that others may not always understand. However, just because a life has been committed to serving God's people, no matter how far that commitment takes you, the devil's harassment is there. In yet another encounter, I found an urgent need to get clarification directly from the Lord.

It was the day I returned home from work, found the lock broken and my front door forced opened. Never before, in travels throughout the country I had no attempted robberies; no burglar had ever invaded my residence.

With caution, I eased my way through the door, stepped over broken glass and prepared to scream and run, if the burglars were still present. Inside the house, the sinister emptiness felt unusually cold; total disarray was in every room.

It felt like my heart sank, my breath became stifled and except for a few clothes, all I owned had been stolen. I thought of the money for my fare home, and with dismay I wondered, *how can I replace this money—at any time soon?*

The thieves had ripped up my mattress, slashed luggage linings, and took used tennis shoes, handbags and a camera. It was useless for a foreigner to call the police on a Kenyan, because none would come; quite possibly, the police assisted the thieves.

With tear-filled eyes looking up to the ceiling I said, "Lord, where are the *angels that have the charge to watch over me?*"

I heard no answer. Before I could enter in a hand-wringing state, it occurred to me to go and check the closet. So I dragged a chair up to the door; prepared for disappointment, I felt upon the top shelf of the closet, where all handbags had been taken or searched. In astonishment, the clutch purse remained in place.

I fought getting happy too soon, as I climbed down out of the chair and unzipped the side pocket of the purse. All ten thousand shillings were still there. With a deep sigh of relief and a hint of new courage, I walked over to the chest of drawers where a set of binoculars—worth $75 had not been removed.

With sweating hands, I pulled out the first drawer and found the two uncovered money orders. At that point, God answered the question I had earlier asked.

The Lord said, "**The angels were inside of the house blinding the thieves.**"

The thieves had to settle for plunder, but the money that was meant for my airfare home had been hidden from their eyes. Nothing is impossible for God to do. Then I began to think that if a shepherd boy could become the king of Israel, then a Kibera boy could become a God-fearing president in Kenya.

At the onset of the mission, I had asked what was in Africa that required me to leave my family and country. Now I realized that the multiplicity of the need in graphically descriptive terms might not accurately cover the magnitude of the suffering.

It had all been based on God's omnipotence; not man's limitations.

God longs to bring us to blessings far beyond our imagination, cultural and religious differences.

9. CONCLUSION GREAT NEWS FOR THE UNNOTICED

Countless gifts and talents are given by God, and yet, there are places in God which have not been asked for. Imagine! So with that in mind, did you know that you can **not** be disqualified for being used by God? Not even a physical disability can stop you from taking your place where He has planned for you to serve.

Throughout the universe, we can rest assured that God's purpose and plan includes a role for each one of us to fulfill. Economic deprivations, personal short-comings, or even perceived generational curses will not cause your alienation from God. Why not take this story as a challenge? Let your mind be fixed on one thing:

God calls

    He trains and sends

        Asks for no man's recommendation as to

whom He can use.

Among the laity, some spend years as what might be termed a 'bench member' or a 'pew hugger.' As such, they are perceived as untalented, simple or ordinary, with nothing much to offer for various reasons.

If you have found yourself put in such a category, even after spending weeks or months in a **New Members' Class**, then I have great news for you.

Because you might not really 'measure up' in the sight of man, being in such circumstances puts you on God's short list to be of value. He is searching for those whose voicemail may not be full or whose time is not tightly scheduled.

Jesus paid close attention to the lowly and simple people; He spoke of how God will move in behalf of the weak and disadvantaged. How did He use a no-name man to give him an important role in Christian History? The man may have been unknown; still, Jesus knew:

    A) The village in which he traveled;
    B) What the man would be carrying;
    C) Where he was going.

This ordinary man was given an unexpected opportunity to do an extra-ordinary service for the Lord.

"... Go ye into the City, and there shall meet you a man bearing a pitcher of water: follow him."
Mark 14:13 (AKJV)

Jesus told His disciples to follow the man not because of his popularity, riches, or influence. The disciples were to follow one (of low profile) solely for Jesus' purpose.

When making our commitments to the Lord, caution is needed because there is a way which **will forfeit** our call to serve. If a revelation is given which could immediately propel us into greatness, rather than to offer a surrendered life to God for His plan, we must take a closer look; the **devil's fingerprints may be all over it.**

Jesus said, **"Take my yoke upon you, and learn of me;... ?** Matt. 11:29.

Just what were we to learn? It is to obey God—Jesus was obedient unto death; and to glorify the Father in all things.

Here are a few questions to ponder as you move towards your destiny.

1. What if your personal mission takes you outside the boundaries of your church walls? Your country?
2. Will your anchor hold when prophecy given to you is contrary to what you feel that God is saying?
3. Would you be willing to sever ties that you have long depended on, and move by faith onto unfamiliar ground?
4. How would it affect your faith if no credit is given for work you have done?
5. Are you willing to have God prune away 'denominational' prejudices?

"May be able to comprehend with all saints what is the breadth, and length, and depth, and height; And to know the love of Christ, which passeth knowledge, that ye might be filled with all the fullness of God."
Eph. 3:18,19 (AKJV)

Once we have grasped the boundless love of God, our fears and doubts will surely dissipate and it will lead us into a powerful and victorious life.

Whether it is a domestic or a foreign assignment, we can be certain that God keeps accurate records for what is done to bring some measure of ease to the less fortunate. **You can make a difference; be of valuable service to God's people—wherever there is a need.** In all, our goal should be to glorify God and Him alone. Here are some suggestions which may help:

1. Get deliverance from *'they say,'* or *'what will they think about me?'*
2. Learn to love without respect to race or nationality.
3. Abandon the practice of pre-judging traditions of others.
4. Ask God to train you to love and appreciate all people

(there are no prerequisites to like or adopt their practices.)
5. Unlearn the need for others to agree with **your** way.
6. Avoid the 'what if' and always focus on obedience.

The ever-faithful Loving Savior is calling for willing, wholehearted people; our rejoicing comes after we have struggled against all odds to let His will be done. Without a willing and obedient heart, it is much easier to become distracted, especially if the path we are to take may be one that is NOT well traveled.

Unaware, we can sometimes have faith and unbelief at the same time. You can be certain that God is able to do all things, but simply can't imagine that He will use YOUR life to model His love to others.

It is so possible. As long as we continue to remember that God looks at the heart, and through Christ, we are new creatures. Let us be about our Father's business.

The language of the heart needs no interpretation.

APPENDIX

All scripture quotations and references, unless other stated, are taken from the Authorized King James Version, 1994: Zondervan Publishing House, Grand Rapids, Michigan 49530

1. Chapter 1 (pg.1): Isaiah 55:8, 9—"For my thoughts are not your thoughts, neither are your ways my ways, saith the Lord. For as the heavens are higher than the earth, so are my ways higher than your ways, and my thoughts than your thoughts.
2. Chapter I (pg. 5): Proverbs 14:12—"There is a way which seemeth right unto man, but the end thereof are the ways of death."
3. Chapter 1 (pg. 8): Isaiah 6:8—"Also I heard the voice of the Lord, saying, Whom shall I send, and who will go for us? Then said I, here am I; send me."
4. Chapter 4 (pg.38): Psalm 25:4—"Show me thy ways, O Lord; teach me thy paths."
5. Chapter 4 (pg. 59): Isaiah 50:5—"The Lord God hath opened mine ear, and I was not rebellious, neither turned away back."
6. Chapter 7 (pg.94): 2 Corinthians 13:11—"When I was a child, I spake as a child, I understood as a child, I thought as a child: but when I became a man, I put away childish things."

7. Chapter 7 (pg. 95): Psalm 145:3—"Great is the Lord, and greatly to be praised; and his greatness is unsearchable."
8. Chapter 8 (pg. 102): Genesis 1:28—"And God blessed them, and God said unto them, Be fruitful, and multiply, and replenish the earth, and subdue it; and have dominion over the fish of the sea, and over the fowl of the air, and over every living thing that moveth upon the earth."
9. Chapter 9 (pg.108): Mark 14:13—"And he sendeth forth two of his disciples, and saith unto them, Go ye into the city, and there shall meet you a man bearing a pitcher of water: follow him."
10. Chapter 9 (pg. 108): Matthew 11:29—"Take my yoke upon you, and learn of me; for I am meek and lowly in heart: and ye shall find rest unto your souls."
11. Chapter 9 (pg. 109): Ephesians 3:18, 19—"May be able to comprehend with all saints what is the breadth, and length, and depth, and height; And to know the love of Christ, which passeth knowledge, that ye might be filled with all the fullness of God."

About the Author

Evangelist Margaret Allen's call to serve came in the form of a scriptural revelation when she was six-years-old. This was given at a time when she had not known **how** God speaks or that He would even speak to a child. Fourteen years later, she had received Christ as head of her life and began an 18-month mission training in Oahu, Hawaii and several years of experience in the mainland assisting pioneering pastors.

Thereafter, her personal work extended to Germany, Spain and Africa. Destined to fulfill an intricate role in Kenya, with a taskforce that was hand-picked by God, she served as a headmistress of an elementary school, where she created an educational sponsorship program. She also trained women in handcrafts and marketed the products, in order to provide a way for destitute families to have food and clothing.

Along with a Kenyan pastor, she was co-founder of a 200-member English-speaking fellowship, Nairobi Gospel Center (NGC), and taught throughout Kenya. Homeland areas included California, Texas, Missouri, Arkansas and Louisiana, where she has ministered as guest speaker and seminar leader. Currently, she spearheads the launching of One Accord Freedom Ministries, an outreach organization that first began in Kenya.

Printed in the United States
31356LVS00005B/499-561